Women and Crime

Women and Crime

Rita James Simon
University of Illinois

Lexington Books
D.C. Heath and Company
Lexington, Massachusetts
Toronto   London

Library of Congress Cataloging in Publication Data

Simon, Rita James.
　　Women and crime.

　　Bibliography: p. 121.
　　Includes index.
　　1. Female offenders—United States. 2. Criminal justice, Administration of—United States. I. Title.
HV6791.S54　　　364.3'74'0973　　　74-25067
ISBN 0-669-97428-5

Second printing July 1976

Published simultaneously in Canada

Printed in the United States of America

International Standard Book Number: 0-669-97428-5

Library of Congress Catalog Card Number: 74-25067

For Julian, and for David, Judith, and Daniel

Contents

List of Tables

Acknowledgements

The author acknowledges with thanks the help and useful advice offered by Navin Sharma, Betty Kordick, Debi Anthony, and Alan Taylor. The facilities provided by the Institute of Communications Research at the University of Illinois greatly facilitated my work on this manuscript.

Introduction

This book describes the extent and type of female involvement in crime in the United States. It presents statistics describing trends in the proportion of women who have been arrested, convicted, sentenced, and paroled over the past two decades. It compares the types of crimes in which women have been most visible. It considers the relationship between the extent of female participation in the labor force at various levels with the anticipated participation of women in the criminal labor market.

The first section reviews the literature on women in crime. It notes the lack of attention that the topic has received in the basic and standard texts in criminology, and it summarizes the major themes in the research that has been done in this area. The other two chapters in this section summarize the current status that women occupy in society as represented by the extent and quality of their participation in the labor force, their marriage and fertility patterns, their incomes and education; these chapters also review the major objectives and goals of the contemporary women's movement. This section also provides a framework for the subsequent analysis of women's participation in criminal activities.

The second section describes women's participation in crime and the treatment women receive at various stages in the criminal justice process. The first chapter compares the proportion of women as opposed to men who have been arrested over the past two decades, and breaks down the types of crimes for which they have been arrested. The next chapter follows women into the courtroom and reports the proportion of women as opposed to men who have been convicted for the same types of offenses. Unlike the statistics on arrests, which have the advantages of uniformity and continuity, information about how women fare at the hands of judges and juries is spottier and less uniform. There are some federal data that describe the proportion of women convicted by types of offenses and some judicial data for California and Ohio. None of the court records extend as far back as the arrest statistics. At best, we can examine trends for a decade. In chapter 6, women are followed out of the courtroom, and the proportion sentenced to prison is compared against the proportion of men. Statistics describing the proportions of men and women inmates are available for at least two and a half decades; but only a few states describe the types of crimes for which men and women have been sentenced. Chapter 7 compares the relative likelihoods that men and women will receive favorable parole hearings. While the parole statistics do not extend back in time far enough to establish longitudinal trends, they do characterize the relative success of female as opposed to male parolees, taking into account the types of offenses, prior criminal records, and history of drug and alcohol use.

The arrest, court, prison, and parole statistics provide the bulk of the empirical data out of which we reconstruct the past, describe the present, and try to project the future profile of the female offender. A brief chapter describing British criminal and penal statistics is also included in this section. An appendix at the end of the volume compares over-all crime rates with female arrest rates for different types of offenses in about twenty-five nations.

The third section summarizes interviews with trial court criminal judges and prosecuting attorneys concerning their images of female offenders, their treatment of women who are involved in crime, and their expectations about the future. It reviews their responses to questions such as: Do you anticipate changes in your own behavior toward female offenders? Do you expect to see women of different backgrounds increasing their contacts with the law? Do you anticipate changes in the types of offenses that women are likely to commit? And, finally, do you expect to have more contacts with more women in the future than you have had in the past?

1 Women in Crime: A Brief Review

Perhaps the most comprehensive statement one can make about the phenomenon of female criminality in the United States is that it has been almost completely ignored by criminologists, lawyers, penologists, and social scientists. In 1968, David Ward observed:

It is not surprising that criminology textbook writers have been able to cover the available knowledge about female criminality in one chapter or less. Our knowledge of the character and causes of female criminality is at the same stage of development that characterized our knowledge of male criminality some 30 or more years ago [Ward 1968, p. 847].

There are two major reasons for a book on women in crime at this time. One is to organize and interpret the statistics and observations that have been accumulating over several decades in order to assess the proportions of women who have engaged in various types of crimes, and to examine how they have been treated by the police, the courts, and prison officials. The second reason is in order to make some prognosis about the future. If one assumes that the changes in women's roles, in their perceptions of self, and in their desire for expanded horizons that began in the latter part of the sixties will not be abated, either by external events such as a major economic depression or by internal processes whereby women examine their situation and decide that their happiness lies in the traditional pursuits of homemaking, wifely companionship, and motherhood, then we would expect that one of the major by-products of the women's movement will be a higher proportion of women who pursue careers in crime. We would also expect changes in the particular types of crimes to which they will be attracted, and in the roles they will perform within the criminal subculture.

As women become more liberated from hearth and home and become more involved in full-time jobs, they are more likely to engage in the types of crimes for which their occupations provide them with the greatest opportunities. They are also likely to become partners and entrepreneurs in crime to a greater extent than they

1

have in the past. Traditionally, women in criminal activity have played subservient roles. They have worked under the direction and guidance of men — their lovers, husbands, or pimps. In most instances, their job was to entice victims, to distract or look out for the police, to carry the loot, or to provide the necessary cover. As a function both of expanded consciousness, as well as occupational opportunities, women's participation, roles, and involvement in crime are expected to change and increase.

But the increase will not be uniform or stable across crimes. Women's participation in financial and white collar offenses [fraud, embezzlement, larceny, and forgery] should increase as their opportunities for employment in higher status occupations expand. Women's participation in crimes of violence, especially homicide and manslaughter, are not expected to increase. The reasoning here is that women's involvement in such acts typically arises out of the frustration, the subservience, and the dependency that have characterized the traditional female role. Case histories of women who kill reveal that one pattern dominates all others. When women can no longer contain their frustrations and their anger, they express themselves by doing away with the cause of their condition, most often a man, sometimes a child. As women's employment and educational opportunities expand, their feelings of being victimized and exploited will decrease, and their motivation to kill will become muted.

A second major purpose of this book, then, is to examine whether such an increase in female participation in financial and white collar offenses has already occurred and, if it has, to report how law enforcement officials at various levels of authority, from police to prosecuting attorneys to judges, have been responding and are planning to respond to it.

Why Do Women Commit Crimes?

Experts representing various disciplines who have written about why men pursue criminal careers have developed a panoply of explanations for man's desire or need to engage in antisocial and illegal behavior. Social, biological, economic, and psychological explanations combined in various ways have been used to develop theories for explaining criminality among men. The complexity of these theories is in sharp contrast to the relatively simple and often single causal explanations that have been offered by experts for explaining women's participation in crime. In this section we review briefly some of those explanations.

Traditionally, most writers on the subject of women in crime have traced female criminality to biological and/or psychological sources with little or no discussion of such social-structural considerations as the state of the economy, occupational and educational opportunities, divisions of labor based on sex roles, and differential associations.

Freudian theory has carried considerable weight. In brief, it claims that women who are not passive, who are not content with their roles as mothers and wives, are maladjusted. The source of their maladjustment is penis envy. In the words of Kate Millet: "[Freud's] entire psychology of women, from which all of modern psychology and psychoanalysis derives heavily, is built upon an original tragic experience—born female. To be born female is to be born castrated" [Millet 1968, p. 180].

Given this basic assumption, Freud explained manifestations of deviance in women, whether they were expressed by a desire for a career, a lack of interest in marriage and/or motherhood, or participation in criminal acts, by the presence in such women of a "masculinity complex." Evidence for the existence of the masculinity complex is manifest by the woman's pursuit of masculine goals: success and recognition in the occupational sphere, power, and money.

According to Freud, all women experience penis envy to some degree. But that which differentiates the "adjusted" from the "maladjusted" woman, the woman who has accepted and internalized the values associated with her role in society from the woman who has not, is that the adjusted woman seeks to compensate for the lack of a penis through the sex act and through motherhood. Devious ways of compensating for the lack of a penis are attending universities, pursuing an autonomous or independent course in life, or joining feminist movements. Freud labeled women who engaged in such behavior "immature," "incomplete," or cases of "arrested development."

Irrespective of the particular social structure or the sociopolitical values that prevailed in the society in which women were reared, Freud identified the female personality as having three basic traits: passivity, masochism, and narcissism. He saw these characteristics as organic. From these characteristics he and many of his followers developed a view of the feminine personality [feminine in Freud's view is identical with female, and masculine with male] as having a lower moral sense and a greater capacity for jealousy. The female's sense of inferiority, rooted as it is in penis envy, generalizes to cultural and intellectual spheres. It follows that women have not contributed much to civilization, to the arts, and to science, because they are incapable of doing so. "She is largely without moral sense, she has little perception of justice, is more subject to emotional bias in judgement and contributes nothing to high culture" [Millet 1968, pp. 200-201].

Lest our readers assume that these beliefs and assumptions died with Victorian or pre World War I society, he or she need only read chapters about the nuclear family, sex roles, or socialization in texts in sociology that were written and widely disseminated as late as the mid-1960s. If the authors of the texts were structural functionalists [and functionalism has been a major sociological perspective since the early 1940s], then the reader would find that the desirable and appropriate roles for women described are consistent with the Freudian model. The functionalists differ from the Freudians in the origins of their explanations. Freud and the Freudians have argued that sexual temperament is a function primarily of biology and genetics. Sexual statuses and sex roles are fixed entities; culture is based upon anatomy. Personality characteristics are not the result of individual choices or social conditions, nor are they the result of the interaction of any of these conditions; but rather they are the product of "a childhood biography imposed upon an inherent constitution by parental behavior" [Millet 1973, p. 203].

Functionalists, of course, recognize the importance of culture and social structure, but conclude, nevertheless, that a division of labor has the greatest utility with men pursuing instrumental goals in the occupational, political, and economic spheres, and women engaging in social-emotional and expressive activities within the family. Inevitably, in both the Freudian and functionalist perspectives, analyses that may start out as descriptive soon take on prescriptive, or value-laden, tones; and actors who deviate from the "normal" modes are characterized as maladjusted and dangerous to themselves and to the stability of the social system.

An eminent neo-Freudian, Erik Erikson, disclaims that his intent is to "down" women or "to deny them the equivalence of individuality and equality of citizenship" [Erikson 1968, p. 278]. But because he accepts the basic Freudian view of the female as biologically inferior, incomplete, and suffering, he wants to help her avoid the inevitable disappointments that would arise should she make the mistake of trying to compete in male enterprises.

Certainly, prior to the 1960s almost everyone who tried to explain why women commit crimes was influenced by the Freudian perspective. This influence is clearly manifest in the frequency with which the following explanations are offered: women who commit crimes do so because they are maladjusted; women turn to crime as a form of rebellion against their "natural" feminine roles. Women who cannot overcome their sense of loss in not having a penis, and who therefore cannot deal with their feelings of inferiority, are traumatized. They grow up envious and in search of revenge. Sometimes the envy and desire for revenge gets channeled into feminist movements and intellectual pursuits. But more often, because they lack the education or professional training or because their family is dependent upon them for economic support these feelings manifest themselves in more antisocial forms of rebellion and aggression. But the root of all these desires is the longing to compensate for the lack of a penis.

Klein [1973] states that Caesar Lombrozo was one of the earliest criminologists to theorize about why women commit crimes. Lombrozo concluded that individuals develop differentially within sexual and racial limitations, and they differ hierarchically from the most highly developed, the white man, to the most primitive, the nonwhite woman. According to Lombrozo:

Women have many traits in common with children: their moral sense is deficient; they are revengeful, jealous. . . . . In ordinary cases these defects are neutralized by piety, maternity, want of passion, sexual coldness, weakness, and an undeveloped intelligence [Klein 1973, p. 10].

Lombrozo explained that women have participated in such a small proportion of criminal behavior because they lack intelligence. Women who do engage in crime are more masculine than are their conformist sisters. He also claimed: "The anomalies of skill, physiognomy, and training capacity of female criminals more closely approximate that of the man, normal or criminal, than they do those of the normal woman" [Klein 1973, p. 10].

Writing as recently as 1966, Rose Giallombardo characterized the image of the woman offender: "Women who commit criminal offenses tend to be regarded as erring and misguided creatures who need protection and help rather than as dangerous criminals from whom members of society should be protected" [p. 7].

The theme of the woman offender as a pathetic creature characterized much of the writing of criminologists and social reformers in the 1930s. Eleanor and Sheldon Glueck's studies of adult and juvenile delinquents viewed women from this perspective. In 1934 the Gluecks wrote:

The women are themselves on the whole a sorry lot. The major problem involved in the delinquency and criminality of our girls is their lack of control of their sexual impulses. Illicit sex practices are extremely common among them, beginning surprisingly early and carry in them brain disease, illegitimacy and unhappy matrimony. . . . When we consider the family background of our women we should rather marvel that a sizeable faction of them, by one influence or another, abandoned their misbehavior, than that so many of them continued their delinquencies [Glueck and Glueck 1934, p. 96].

From the five hundred delinquent women studied in Massachusetts in 1934, the Gluecks prepared the following list of offenses that their respondents had committed prior to their commitment.

Cause of First Known Arrest

Offense	Percent
1. Offense against person	1.8
2. Offense against chastity—adultery, polygamy	7.6
3. Offense against chastity—common nightwalking or frequenting a house of ill fame	5.8
4. Offense against chastity—fornication	5.2
5. Offense against chastity—keeping house of ill fame or sharing proceeds of prostitution	1.0
6. Offense against chastity—lewd and lascivious person	18.0
7. Stubborn children (runaway, truancy, waywardness, breaking glass, unnatural act)	20.2
8. Against family and children	2.4
9. Against public health, safety, and policy (except drink and drug)	16.2
10. Drink	9.0
11. Drugs	0.4
12. Against Property	12.4
Total	100.0
	(500)

More than 80 percent of these women committed acts of sexual or personal immorality; and only 12.4 percent committed antisocial, illegal acts that did not involve sex or immorality. Other characteristics that these women shared were that 68 percent had venereal disease before they were twenty one, 42 percent "had the habit of drinking," 54 percent had had "illegitimate pregnancies," 68 percent had had eight years of schooling or less, and 72 percent were of "dull intelligence or less." [Glueck and Glueck 1934].

In their policy recommendations, the Gluecks emphasized: "The obvious improvement in the procedures of criminal justice, though clearly called for, will probably contribute disappointingly little to a solution of the manifold problems presented by crime" [Glueck and Glueck 1934, p. 308].

Although warning against the dangers involved, they nevertheless advocated voluntary sterilization as an advisable and possible mode of preventative treatment and an extension of the juvenile court procedure and philosophy. They recommended the latter because "these types of women need just as much protection and salvation as children; many of them are, in fact, psychologically children in their incapacity for assuming social responsibilities" [Glueck and Glueck 1934, p. 318]. They also urged the establishment of sentencing bodies staffed by psychiatrists, sociologists, educators, and lawyers with the power to hand down "indeterminate sentences."

Otto Pollak's book *The Criminality of Women,* [1950,] was important, because it challenged basic assumptions concerning the extent and quality of women's involvement in criminal behavior. Essentially, Pollak argued that women have been commended and praised for their drastic underrepresentation in criminal activities but, in fact, they do not deserve such praise. According to Pollak, women's participation in crime has not been significantly lower than that of men's; rather [1] the types of crimes women commit are less likely to be detected; [2] even when detected, they are less likely to be reported; for example, shoplifting, domestic theft, and theft by prostitutes; and [3] even when crimes are reported, women still have a much better chance than do men of avoiding arrest or conviction because of the double standard employed by law enforcement officials which is favorable to women.

Pollak also claimed that even when women commit visible offenses, they are less likely to be apprehended, because their male victims are too embarrassed or too chivalrous to report the act. When a man and a woman team up to commit crimes, the man is the one likely to get caught and punished, because he is usually the active partner. The man gets caught because he engages in the overt act. Women usually play the role of instigator, motivator, or arranger. Chivalry prevents the man from involving his female counterpart.

For the three reasons cited above, Pollak contends that the greater conformity of women as opposed to men is a myth. To explode that myth, men [those who are accused of crime as well as law enforcement officials] must change their perceptions, their attitudes, and their behavior towards women. Only then will the true magnitude of women's participation in crime be apparent.

Pollak's work did not stimulate a new generation of criminologists to reconsider the roles and frequency of women in crime. It did not even succeed in getting "women" or "females" into the indexes of basic texts on criminology. Indeed, Pollak's work may be more important in the 1970s as a result of the women's movement than it was at the time of its publication. But any review of the literature of women in crime must recognize it as a major work, not only because it has so little competition, but because Pollak was the first writer to insist that women's participation in crime is indeed commensurate to their representation in the population and to the frequency of crime committed by men.

In the two decades since its publication, there has been no scholarly and empirical treatment of the problem. There has been some work on delinquent girls which reflected Pollak's interest [Cowie, Cowie, and Slater 1968; Vedder and Somerville 1966; and Konopka 1966], but most of the books about women in crime have either dealt with the social relations of women in prisons or have been of the exotic case history genre.

Between 1965 and 1971, at least three case history studies were published: *Women in Crime* [Parker 1965], *How Could She Do That* [de Rham 1969], *Women Who Murder* [Sparrow 1970], and earlier, *Six Criminal Women* [Jenkins 1949]. Each of them accept as fact Pollak's assumption that women commit many more crimes for which they are never arrested than do men and that the legitimate and traditional roles women perform in society provide excellent cover for the most devious types of crimes. In each of these case history studies, the woman as nurse, lover, companion, secretary or wife carefully and slowly poisons to death the person with whose life she has been entrusted. What finally brings her to the attention of the law? Usually, the diligence of an insurance investigator [shades of *Double Indemnity*] or the suspicion of someone who was in a position to notice that over a decade, sweet, timid Mrs. X has buried three husbands, each of whom left her a substantial estate, or someone has become aware that kind, patient Nurse G has substantially improved her financial situation as a result of inheriting the major portions of estates of elderly widows whom she attended until their deaths.

These studies strive to dramatize Pollak's basic assumption that women are no more endowed with morality and decency than are men; but the roles they perform in society assume goodness, charity, and morality, and it is those roles that serve as useful masks for hiding criminal activities. It is important to emphasize that Pollak, Parker, Jenkins, de Rham, Sparrow, and other authors do not claim that women are more bloodthirsty or venomous than men, but rather that the roles men traditionally perform do not provide them with such appropriate masks. When a man commits a crime, it is more likely to be a public act than when a woman does.

In 1967, Reckless and Kay reviewed the various explanations offered for the low proportion of female involvement in criminal behavior and concluded:

Perhaps the most important factor in determining reported and acted-upon violational behavior of women is the chivalry factor. Victims or observers of female violators are unwilling to take action against the offenders because she is a woman. Police are much less willing to make on-the-spot arrests of or "book" and hold women for court action than men. Courts are also easy on women, because they are women. . . . Overlooking, letting-go, excusing, unwillingness to report and to hold, being easy on women are part of the differential handling of the adult females in the law enforcement process from original complaint to admission to prison. The differential law enforcement handling seems to be built into our basic attitudes toward women [p. 16].

2

The Contemporary Women's Movement

The contemporary women's movement was born in the latter part of the decade that saw the rise of a civil rights movement and a student-led antiwar movement. Many of those who participated in both of these movements became leaders and organizers of various branches of the women's movement. In part, the experiences of the younger women in the politics of the New Left served as the spawning ground for their consciousness of the need to liberate themselves and their sisters. What these women learned was that even among men who were radical in many of their political and social beliefs, who believed in equality among the races, who advocated major changes in the occupational structure and favored redistribution of income and wealth, that even among these men, women generally, and they in particular, were treated as second-class citizens. They were expected to serve as handmaidens, as bearers and servers, and as bed companions to men in radical politics whose roles and attitudes toward women were not significantly different from the roles and relations that men with more conservative views and life styles held toward women in the larger society.

Women who were active in the civil-rights movement were struck especially by the similarities between their relationships to men and the relationships that blacks had toward white society. Using the language of the civil rights movement, they could make analogies between a sex-caste system and a caste system that had race as its distinguishing characteristic: blacks were at the bottom of one system; they were at the bottom of the other.

The current array of women's movements, from reform to revolutionary, or from moderate to extreme, has its parallel in earlier women's movements, going back to the period immediately preceding the Civil War and extending up through the 1920s. The National Women's Party (NWP), formerly the Congressional Union, was the more militant group compared with the National American Woman's Suffrage Association (NAWSA) and its successor, the League of Women Voters. The National Women's Party was

11

founded in 1913, the National American Woman's Suffrage Association, in 1890. Until the passage of the Eighteenth Amendment, both movements concentrated their major efforts on the attainment of suffrage. But after 1920, the NWP devoted its efforts to passage of an equal rights amendment. In 1929, one year after suffrage had been attained, Alice Paul, leader of the NWP, minimized the value of the victory by stating: "Women today . . . are still in every way subordinate to men before the law, in the professions, in the church, in industry, and in the home" [Chafe 1972, p. 115].

Leaders of the NWP rejected attempts to form coalitions with other reform or progressive groups that were working for civil rights, disarmament, or improving the lot of the working people. Arguing in much the same vein as the radical women's movement of the 1970s, they reasoned that any expenditure of energy on issues that were extraneous to women's rights would only impede progress toward their major goal: freeing American women from their present condition of enslavement.

The NAWSA, under its new name, the League of Women Voters, pursued the opposite course. They contended that the attainment of suffrage has secured for them their most important and fundamental rights. They joined efforts with other groups for sound government, integrity in public life, and reforms in the economic and social spheres. The league went out of its way to avoid being identified as a lobby for one group only. Chafe quotes Dorothy Strauss, a league leader: "We of the league are very much for the rights of women, but we are not feminists primarily, we are citizens" [Chafe 1972, p. 115].

World War II brought an end both to conflict within the women's movement as well as to the women's movement per se (as it did to most other social-reform movements). It took two decades after the end of the Second World War for the movement to be revived. And like its initial birth and subsequent revival, the contemporary women's movement followed on the heels of another social movement aimed at redressing grievances of blacks and other ethnic minority groups.

Whenever Americans became sensitive to the issue of human rights, it seemed, the women's movement acquired new support in one way or another, and the 1960s proved no exception to the rule. The civil rights movement did not cause the revival of feminism, but it did help to create a set of favorable circumstances [Chafe 1972, p. 233].

Catherine Stimpson described the historical ties that bound blacks' liberation and women's liberation movements together for more than a century [Stimpson 1971, pp. 622-57].[a] She points out that the antislavery movement preceded the first major women's rights movement, that black male suffrage preceded women's suffrage, and that the civil-rights movement of the sixties preceded the contemporary women's liberation movement. Paraphrasing Alva Myrdal, she notes that both blacks and women are highly visible; they cannot hide even if they want to. A patriarchal ideology assigns them both several virtues: blacks are tough; women are fragile. But both are judged to be "naturally inferior" in those respects that carry prestige, power, and advantages in the society. Stimpson quotes Thomas Jefferson:

Even if America were a pure democracy, its inhabitants should keep women, slaves, and babies away from its deliberations. The less education women and Blacks get, the better; manual education is the most they can have. The only right they possess is the right which criminals, lunatics, and idiots share, to love their divine subordination within the paterfamilia and to obey the paterfamilia himself [Stimpson 1971, p. 623].

Women found that men with whom they had worked side by side against slavery, or for civil rights, peace, or the right to organize in trade unions, left them when they sought to gain the same rights for women. The behavior of Henry Stanton vis-à-vis his wife, Elizabeth, and the women's movement of that era is a case in point. The Stantons were both activists in the antislavery movement; but Henry left town when Elizabeth organized the women's rights meeting in Seneca Falls in 1848.

Samuel Gompers and his successors, as heads of the American Federation of Labor (AFL), attacked the presence of married women in the work force and asserted that females should direct their energies toward getting married and raising a family [Chafe 1972]. In 1921, the Women's Trade Union League (WTUL) petitioned its executive council to issue federal charters that would permit women to organize in sexually segregated unions. The AF of L League rejected the petition, and when the women accused the executive council of prejudice, Gompers replied that the AF of L discriminated against "any nonassimilable race" [Chafe 1972, p.

[a]From "Thy Neighbor's Wife, Thy Neighbor's Servants: Women's Liberation and Black Civil Rights," Catherine Stimpson in *Woman in Sexist Society*; Studies in Power and Powerlessness, Vivian Gornick and Barbara K. Moran (Eds.), Basic Books, Inc., New York (1971).

78]. During the Second World War, R. J. Thomas, president of the United Auto Workers, claimed that women accepted the advantages of union membership but not the responsibilities. He predicted that at the end of the war, almost all women would lose their jobs.

The most recent feminists found that they received little interest, attention, or sympathy when they tried to have the discrimination they experienced recognized as a legitimate source of complaint.

Like their ancestors in the antislavery movement,

some women in the civil rights movement felt abused. They were given work supportive in nature and negligible in influence; they were relegated to the research library and to the mimeograph machine . . . . Not only did movement men tend to be personally chauvinistic, but many of the movement's ideals—strength, courage, spirit were those society attributes to masculinity. Women may have those characteristics but never more than men . . . [Stimpson 1971, p. 646].

Stokely Carmichael remarked: "The only position for women in SNCC is prone."

In tracing the founding of the contemporary women's movement, Freeman (1973) cites an incident that she claims precipitated the formation of the "Chicago group," the first independent women's group in the county.

At the August 1967 convention of the *National Conference for New Politics*, a women's caucus had met for days only to be told by the chair that its resolution wasn't significant enough to merit a floor discussion. Only by threatening to tie up the convention with procedural motions, did the women succeed in having their statement tacked on to the end of the agenda. But in the end, their resolution was never discussed. The chair refused to recognize any of the many women standing by the microphones. Instead he recognized someone from the floor to speak on the "forgotten American, the American Indian." Five women rushed to the podium and demanded an explanation. The chairman responded by patting one of them on the head (literally) and saying, "Cool down, little girl. We have more important things to talk about than women's problems [Freeman 1973, pp. 800-801].

Another incident cited by Freeman that also illustrates the lack of empathy that men in the radical politics of the sixties had for women's rights occurred at the University of Washington. An SDS organizer was explaining to a large meeting how white college youth established rapport with the poor whites with whom they were working. He said that sometimes, after analyzing societal ills, the men shared leisure time by "balling a chick together." He pointed out that such acitvities did much to enhance the political consciousness of the poor white youth. A woman in the audience asked, "And what did it do for the consciousness of the chick?" After the meeting, a handful of enraged women formed Seattle's first women's group [Freeman 1973, p. 801].

Women's liberation groups continue to see connections between their status in American society and the status of blacks. In comparing the ideology of the women's movement with that of the blacks, Stimpson observed:

> [The black movement] teaches that the oppressed must become conscious of their oppression, of the debasing folly of their lives, before change can come. Change, if it does come, will overthrow both a class, a social group, and a caste—a social group held in contempt [Stimpson 1971, p. 648].

Stimpson goes on to make perhaps the strongest statement of the contemporary women's movement on the similarities between themselves and blacks:

1) Women, like black slaves, belong to a master. They are property and whatever credit they gain redounds to him.

2) Women, like black slaves, have a personal relationship to the men who are their masters.

3) Women, like blacks, get their identity and status from white men.

4) Women, like blacks, play an idiot role in the theatre of the white man's fantasies. Though inferior and dumb, they are happy, especially when they can join a mixed group where they can mingle with The Man.

5) Women, like blacks, buttress the white man's ego. Needing such support, the white man fears its loss; fearing such loss, he fears women and blacks.

6) Women, like blacks, sustain the white man: "They wipe his ass and breast feed him when he is little, they school him in his youthful years, do his clerical work and raise him and his replacements later, and all through his life in the factories, on the migrant farms, in the restaurants, hospitals, offices, and homes, they sew for him, stoop for him, cook for him, clean for him, sweep, run errands, haul away his garbage, and nurse him when his frail body falters."

7) Women, like blacks, are badly educated. In school they internalize a sense of being inferior, shoddy, and intellectually crippled. In general, the cultural apparatus—the profession of history, for example—ignores them.

8) Women, like blacks, see a Tom image of themselves in the mass media.

9) Striving women, like bourgeois blacks, become imitative, ingratiating, and materialistic when they try to make it in the white man's world.

10) Women, like blacks, suffer from the absence of any serious study on the possibility of real "temperamental and cognitive differences" between the races and sexes [Gornick and Moran 1971, p. 649].

Since the end of the 1960s, many variations of the initial women's movement have emerged. These movements and ideologies range from reformist to revolutionary. NOW (National Organization for Women) is probably the most conservative. Maintaining the civil rights analogy, it is the NAACP of the women's movement. Founded in 1966 by Betty Friedan, it has concentrated most of its efforts on legal and economic problems. Its membership is on the average older than that of the more radical women's groups, but like the more radical groups, it is composed primarily of white, well-educated professional women.

Between the end of the sixties and the early part of the seventies, a variety of women who became disenchanted with, or were thrown out of, New Left or civil rights movements organized FLF (Female Liberation First), WITCH (Women's International Terrorist Conspiracy from Hell), Red Stockings, and the Feminists. The characteristics that distinguish the moderate groups from the more radical ones are the almost exclusive emphases that the former place on job equality and passage of the Equal Rights Amendment; the strategy of working for change within the system through lobbying, court action, and education; and the willingness to accept men as members.

The radical groups consider the entire system corrupt. Their targets are as much the institutions of marriage, the family, and motherhood as unequal opportunities in employment and education. Consciousness raising for these women involves educating their sisters to the belief that every aspect of their relationship with men is exploitative. The Red Stocking Manifesto expresses those sentiments:

Women are an oppressed class. Our oppression is total, affecting every facet of our lives. We are exploited as sex objects, domestic servants, and cheap labor. We are considered inferior beings, whose only purpose is to enhance men's lives. Our humanity is denied. Our prescribed behavior is enforced by the threat of physical violence.

Because we have lived so intimately with our oppressors in isolation from each other, we have been kept from seeing our personal suffering as a political condition. This creates the illusion that a woman's relationship with her man is a matter of interplay between two unique personalities and can be worked out individually. In reality, every such relationship is a class relationship, the conflicts between individual men and women are political conflicts that can only be solved collectively.

We identify the agents of our oppressors as men. Male supremacy is the oldest, most basic form of domination. All other forms of exploitation and oppression (racism, capitalism, imperialism, etc.) are extensions of male supremacy: men dominate women, a few men dominate the rest.

We identify with all women. We define our best interest as that of the poorest, most brutally exploited women. We repudiate all economic, racial, education, or status privileges that divide us from other women [Epstein and Goode 1973, p. 178].

Some women's groups espouse homosexual relationships as a desirable alternative to heterosexual ones. The "feminists," for example, argue that the basic assumption of most women's groups that women's lives will always be intertwined with men's ignores an important option; women might consider living separately from men, to accept homosexual relations as an alternative to heterosexual relationships.

Abbott and Love write:

Recognition of the validity of the lesbian lifestyle and acceptance of lesbian activism in women's liberation is crucial to the women's movement's ultimate goal—a new, harmonious, cooperating, nonauthoritarian society in which men and women are free to be themselves. To end the oppression of the lesbian is to admit of a wider range of being and acting under the generic name "woman". It is a cause that must be undertaken by women's liberation if women are truly to free themselves [Gornick and Moran 1971, p. 621].

For all the ideological differences and tactical variations that exist within the women's movement, the demographic characteristics of their membership are extraordinarily homogeneous. In the main, the movement is led by, appeals to, and has as the large majority of its members young white women who are college educated and whose families are middle and upper-middle class. After they leave the university, most of these women enter professions. None of the groups within the movement has made any noticeable dent on the blue-collar female workers, on black women, or on high-school-educated housewives. The gulf between these types of nonmovement women and the authors of the *Red Stocking Manifesto* may be as great as any that those writers envisage between men and women. How likely it is, therefore, that the women's movement will significantly alter the behaviors, the perceptions, the beliefs, and the life styles of women already involved in criminal careers is still too early to say. But given the characteristics of the members of the women's movement, it is unlikely that it has had a significant impact, or that indeed it has made much of an impression on women already involved in crime. Indeed, most of these women have yet to hear of consciousness raising, and of sisterhood in a political sense; and those who have may well ridicule these sentiments or attack them as the empty mouthings of women whose lives have always been characterized by material comfort, stability, and security.

Millet's observations of how prostitutes behave in court dramatizes the point:

The scene in court is astonishing: the woman is absolutely flirting throughout the whole precedings. She does it when she comes in, she does it when she's going out with the cops and clerks. It doesn't break down for a minute. That interchange is very weird to watch and it's something that would take a long time to explain, but you know the woman's security and advantage lies in maintaining the relationship [Millet 1973, p. 157].

There is one avenue, however, through which the women's movement may already be having a significant impact on women in crime. The movement's rhetoric and activities may serve to alter the treatment that women offenders receive at the hands of the police, prosecutors, and other law enforcement personnel. What we have heard from many police with whom we have talked on this topic is: "If it's equality these women want, we'll see that they get it."

3 American Women: Their Demographic and Status Characteristics

The previous chapter described the aspirations and goals of the women's movement. It examined the social and political context that led to the formation of the contemporary women's movement, and it raised questions concerning the implication of the movement for more extensive and more active participation in conformist and deviant activities on the part of women.

This chapter examines census and other demographic data in order to characterize the extent and type of women's participation in the labor force and to describe patterns and trends concerning marriage, fertility, and education among American women. The major objectives of this chapter are the same as those of the previous one: to assess how these factors—in this instance, demographic and labor force characteristics—are likely to influence women's participation in crime.

The major hypotheses are that increased participation in the labor force provides women with more opportunities for committing certain types of crimes. As those opportunities increase, women's participation in larceny, fraud, embezzlement, and other financial and white-collar crimes should increase. On the other hand, as women enter the labor force in greater proportions, as they acquire more skills through educational and occupational training, and as they receive more generous financial compensation, their sense of frustration, their feelings of being victimized, and their sense of powerlessness should diminish. According to Ward, Reckless, and others who have studied women who have committed crimes of violence, it is these emotions that stimulate women to violence. The full set of expectations, then, are that women's participation in financial and white-collar offenses should increase, and their participation in crimes of violence should decrease, as they gain greater entry into the business world and are rewarded for their contributions.

The 1970 census has the female population in the United States (children and adults) at 105 million. Females outnumber males by about 3.5 million. The proportion of married white and nonwhite women in specific age categories are shown in table 3-1. The figures indicate that from the mid-1960s on, a higher proportion of white women opted to delay marriage until they were at least twenty-five years old; and within all age groups, a higher proportion of nonwhite women have remained unmarried.

Birth rates have dropped since the years immediately following the Second World War, and as of 1972 fertility rates were the lowest ever observed in this country [Blake 1974, p. 42]. Although the number of children American women are having is decreasing, the proportion of women who are opting to remain childless is not increasing. For example, if we look at the percentage childless among college-educated women who are married to men with a college education, we find that the proportion has remained stable at 10 percent since 1940. In a recent review of fertility patterns and attitudinal data about childlessness, Judith Blake concluded: "A willingness to regard childlessness and the only child as desirable or even acceptable is still rare."

In response to a Gallup survey in 1973, 84 percent answered that marriage was happier with children.

An analysis of the census materials, poll data, or a review of experts' interpretations all lead to the conclusion that marriage is no less fashionable in the 1970s than it was in the 1950s and that marriage without children is no more popular today than it was in the days of the baby boom. What is happening demographically is a significant trend toward smaller families. But smaller families do not imply that female socialization is undergoing a basic departure from the traditional pattern.

The phenomenon that appears to be directly related to the preference for smaller families is the propensity for married women to enter and remain in the labor force full time. Table 3-2 indicates that the biggest *increase* in the labor force has occurred among the married women in contrast to the women in the single and divorced/widowed categories. Among the married women, those who have preschool children are less likely to work outside their homes full time than are those whose children are at least six years old. But this pattern of a sharp differentiation in the full-time employment of married women with and without preschool children is not recent. As table 3-3 demonstrates, the differentiation was manifest two and a half decades ago.

Table 3-1
Percentage Married Women by Age and Race: 1950-70

Age	18-19		20-24		25-29		30-34		35-44	
Year	White	Nonwhite	White	Nonwhite	White	Nonwhite	White	Nonwhite	White	Nonwhite
1950			65.6	65.7	83.7	80.2	86.5	83.1	84.8	80.0
1952	31.3	29.8	68.6	69.5	84.4	84.9	87.8	82.8	85.5	79.8
1953	33.1	35.8	68.5	72.4	86.1	82.1	88.5	84.2	86.7	75.6
1957	30.2	27.7	70.2	61.6	87.4	78.3	89.3	85.6	87.5	80.4
1958	33.5	33.3	70.1	61.6	86.2	81.0	89.8	83.5	87.5	80.0
1959	34.1	31.2	70.5	64.5	88.4	83.4	90.0	82.5	87.7	82.2
1960	28.7	24.0	69.7	66.3	88.4	79.5	89.7	82.1	88.0	81.7
1961	27.3	26.3	69.3	63.8	86.6	84.0	89.0	84.7	87.8	83.0
1962	30.3	25.2	69.5	61.4	87.4	81.0	87.9	84.9	88.9	82.4
1963	28.7	25.7	67.5	63.6	88.2	79.5	90.6	84.1	89.1	79.9
1964	27.2	29.0	66.7	64.9	87.1	83.3	92.2	87.9	88.6	83.3
1965	26.6	22.3	66.0	63.0	88.0	81.8	90.9	87.3	88.5	83.9
1966	25.0	28.0	68.6	60.3	87.4	79.1	90.1	86.5	89.1	84.8
1967	23.0	26.7	65.8	59.8	87.3	80.0	90.0	86.0	88.7	81.4
1968	22.9	22.8	62.7	54.3	87.5	75.9	90.1	80.8	88.3	78.8
1969	22.3	22.7	63.8	51.5	86.4	74.1	90.3	80.4	88.5	79.1
1970	22.7	21.5	59.6	51.6	84.0	71.1	87.5	76.6	87.1	76.4

Source: Adapted from Abbott L. Ferris, *Indicators of Trends in the Status of American Women* (New York: Russell Sage Foundation, 1971), Statistics: 1950-1969. *1970 U.S. Census of Population*, Subject Reports (U.S. Department of Commerce, 1973), Statistics: 1970.

Table 3-2

Females in Labor Force as Percentage of All Females, by Marital Status: 1940-70

Year	Total	Single	Married	Widowed/Divorced
1940	27.4	48.1	16.7	32.0
1944	35.0	58.6	25.6	35.7
1947	29.8	51.2	21.4	34.6
1950	31.4	50.5	24.8	36.0
1955	33.5	46.4	29.4	36.0
1956	34.2	46.4	30.2	36.9
1957	34.8	46.8	30.8	37.6
1958	35.0	45.4	31.4	37.9
1959	35.2	43.4	32.3	38.0
1960	34.8	44.1	31.7	37.1
1961	36.8	44.4	34.0	39.0
1962	35.7	41.7	33.7	36.6
1963	3..	41.0	34.6	35.8
1964	35..	40.9	34.4	36.1
1965	36.7	40.5	35.7	35.7
1966	37..	40.8	35.4	36.4
1967	39.7	50.7	37.8	35.9
1968	40.7	51.3	38.3	35.8
1969	41.6	51.2	39.6	35.8
1970	42.6	53.0	41.4	36.2

Source: Adapted from Abbott L. Ferris, *Indicators of Trends in the Status of American Women* (New York: Russell Sage Foundation, 1971), Statistics: 1940-1969. *1970 U.S. Census of Population*, Subject Reports (U.S. Department of Commerce, 1973), Statistics: 1970.

Closer analysis of the types of employment in which women are engaged indicates that the occupational patterns are still based on a sex-role definition that has women performing in service-like roles and in jobs that involve less initiative and responsibility than those occupied by men. Table 3-4 shows the distribution of men and women in four major occupational categories. Two characteristics stand out. First, the relative distribution of men and women across the four occupational categories has remained stable since 1948. There have been no major shifts in the types of employment men and women have engaged in for the past quarter of a century. Second, the majority of women were in 1948, and are in 1971, employed in white-collar positions. But "white collar" is a broad category that includes professional and managerial positions as well as clerical and sales personnel. The former positions carry with them higher prestige, greater authority, and usually higher financial rewards than

Table 3-3

Employed Married Women as Percentage of All Women with Children of Various Ages: 1948-70

Year	No children under 18	Children 6-17 (none under 6)	Children under 6	Children under 6 and between 6-17
1948	28.4	26.0	9.2	12.7
1949	28.7	27.3	10.0	12.2
1950	30.3	28.3	11.2	12.6
1951	31.0	30.3	13.6	14.6
1952	30.9	31.3	13.7	14.1
1953	31.2	32.2	15.8	15.2
1954	31.6	33.2	14.3	15.5
1955	32.7	34.7	15.1	17.3
1956	35.3	36.6	15.9	16.1
1957	35.6	36.6	15.9	17.9
1958	35.4	37.6	18.4	18.1
1959	35.2	39.8	18.3	19.0
1960	34.7	39.0	18.2	18.9
1961	37.3	41.7	19.6	20.3
1962	36.1	41.8	21.1	21.5
1963	37.4	41.5	22.4	22.5
1964	37.8	43.0	23.6	21.9
1965	38.3	42.7	23.8	22.8
1966	38.4	43.7	24.0	24.3
1967	38.9	45.0	26.9	26.2
1968	40.1	46.9	27.8	27.4
1969	41.0	48.6	29.3	27.8
1970	42.2	49.2	30.3	30.5

Source: Adapted from Abbott L. Ferris, *Indicators of Trends in the Status of American Women* (New York: Russell Sage Foundation, 1971), p. 373, Statistics: 1948-1969. *1970 U.S. Census of Population,* Subject Reports (U.S. Department of Commerce, 1973), Statistics: 1970.

do the latter. The crucial question then is: Among the men and women who are employed in white-collar positions, what percentage are in professional and managerial categories and what percentage are in clerical and sales?

The story unfolds in table 3-5. In 1971, twice as many men were in professional and managerial positions as were in clerical and sales. Among the women, the proportions were almost exactly the reverse; slightly more than twice as many were in clerical and sales positions as were in professional and managerial positions. In 1948, approximately one out of five men and women among those employed as white-collar workers were professionals. In 1971, slightly more than one out of three men were so employed compared with

Table 3-4

Percentage Distribution of Employed Workers, by Sex: 1948-71

| Year | White Collar | | Blue Collar | | Service Workers | | Farm Workers | |
	Male	Female	Male	Female	Male	Female	Male	Femal
1948	30.8	49.3	47.7	22.2	6.1	20.5	15.4	8.0
1949	31.8	49.9	46.2	21.0	6.4	21.3	15.6	7.8
1950	32.1	50.4	46.8	20.6	6.4	22.0	14.7	6.9
1951	31.0	50.2	49.5	21.8	6.1	21.4	13.4	6.6
1952	31.8	51.6	49.1	21.4	6.0	21.1	13.1	5.9
1953	32.5	51.0	48.8	21.9	6.5	21.9	12.3	5.2
1954	33.2	52.4	48.1	20.1	6.2	22.0	12.5	5.6
1955	33.1	51.9	48.4	19.4	6.1	22.5	12.4	6.3
1956	33.5	52.1	48.3	18.6	6.4	23.1	11.9	6.2
1957	34.7	53.3	47.9	18.2	6.4	22.9	11.1	5.6
1958	36.5	55.1	46.8	17.0	6.4	23.3	10.3	4.6
1959	36.7	54.9	47.0	16.8	6.3	23.5	10.0	4.7
1960	37.4	55.3	46.6	16.6	6.5	23.7	9.6	4.4
1961	38.0	55.6	46.0	16.3	6.7	24.2	9.3	3.9
1962	38.5	56.0	46.1	16.3	6.7	24.0	8.7	3.6
1963	38.2	55.8	46.9	16.5	6.9	24.1	8.0	3.5
1964	38.4	56.2	47.0	16.7	7.0	23.9	7.6	3.3
1965	38.3	57.0	47.7	16.7	6.9	23.2	7.1	3.1
1966	38.6	57.6	48.0	17.1	7.1	22.7	6.4	2.6
1967	39.0	48.4	47.4	16.9	7.0	22.3	6.2	2.3
1968	39.7	59.1	47.7	17.1	6.9	21.8	6.0	2.1
1969	40.1	59.4	47.7	17.1	6.7	21.6	5.6	2.0
1970	41.9	60.5	47.0	16.0	6.7	21.7	5.3	1.8
1971	41.0	61.1	45.3	14.9	8.3	22.3	5.4	1.7

Source: Adapted from Abbott L. Ferris, *Indicators of Trends in the Status of American Women* (New York: Russell Sage Foundation, 1971), pp. 374, 376, 378, 389, Statistics: 1948-1969. *1972 Statistical Abstract of the U.S.* (Washington, D.C.: U.S. Department of Commerce, Bureau of the Census, 1972), table 366, p. 230, Statistics: 1970-1971.

slightly more than one out of four women. In the managerial category, in 1948 the proportions were slightly more than four out of ten men compared to one out of ten women. In 1971, the proportion among the men remained relatively stable at slightly more than three and a half out of ten; but among the women, the proportion dropped from one out of ten to a little more than one out of fifteen.

These figures tell a dramatic story. Even though women's overall representation in the labor force during this same time span (roughly 1948 to 1971) has increased by 40 percent, their participation in positions of authority, prestige, and higher monetary rewards has not kept pace with that increase. In 1948, 29 percent of the women employed in white-collar positions occupied professional and managerial slots; in 1971, the percentage increased to 33.

Table 3-5
White-Collar Employment: Males and Females as Percentage of All Employed Males and Females: 1948-71

Year	All White Collar Jobs		Professional and Technical		Managers and Officials		Clerical		Sales Workers	
	Male	Female	Male	Female	Male	Female	Male	Female	Male	Female
1948	30.8	49.3	5.8	9.0	12.9	5.2	6.9	26.9	5.3	8.2
1949	31.8	49.9	6.0	9.2	13.2	5.5	6.9	27.0	5.6	8.2
1950	32.1	50.4	6.4	10.3	12.9	5.7	7.2	26.3	5.6	8.2
1951	31.0	50.2	7.0	9.8	12.2	5.7	6.3	27.0	5.5	7.6
1952	31.8	51.6	7.5	10.2	12.2	5.4	6.6	28.5	5.4	7.5
1953	32.5	51.0	8.0	10.7	12.7	5.1	6.4	27.5	5.4	7.7
1954	33.2	52.4	8.4	10.9	12.4	5.1	6.7	28.5	5.8	7.9
1955	33.1	51.9	8.3	11.0	12.6	5.0	6.5	28.1	5.7	7.7
1956	33.5	52.1	8.7	10.8	12.5	4.9	6.6	28.6	5.6	7.8
1957	34.7	53.3	9.3	11.4	12.9	4.9	6.8	29.4	5.8	7.6
1958	36.5	55.1	10.4	12.3	13.6	5.0	6.8	30.1	5.7	7.7
1959	36.7	54.9	10.5	12.1	13.5	5.1	6.8	29.9	5.8	7.9
1960	37.4	55.3	10.9	12.4	13.6	5.0	7.1	30.3	5.8	7.7
1961	38.0	55.6	11.4	12.4	13.8	5.1	7.1	30.5	5.8	7.6
1962	38.5	56.0	11.7	12.7	14.2	5.0	7.1	30.8	5.5	7.5
1963	38.2	55.8	11.9	12.8	13.8	4.8	7.0	30.9	5.5	7.3
1964	38.4	56.2	12.0	13.0	13.9	4.7	7.0	31.2	5.5	7.3
1965	38.3	57.0	12.1	13.3	13.4	4.5	7.1	31.8	5.7	7.5
1966	38.6	57.6	12.4	13.4	13.3	4.5	7.1	32.6	5.7	7.2
1967	39.0	58.4	13.0	13.7	13.3	4.4	7.2	33.2	5.5	7.1
1968	39.4	59.1	13.4	13.9	13.6	4.5	7.1	33.8	5.7	6.9
1969	40.1	59.4	13.8	13.8	13.8	4.3	7.0	34.3	5.5	6.9
1970	41.0	60.5	14.0	14.5	14.2	4.5	7.1	34.5	5.6	7.0
1971	41.0	61.1	14.0	15.0	14.5	4.9	7.0	34.0	6.0	7.2

Source: Adapted from Abbott L. Ferris, *Indicators of Trends in the Status of American Women* (New York: Russell Sage Foundation, 1971), p. 374. *Statistics: 1948-1969. 1972 Statistical Abstract of the U.S.* (Washington, D.C.: U.S. Department of Commerce, Bureau of the Census, 1972), table 366, p. 230, Statistics: 1970-1971.

Table 3-6

High-School and College Graduates by Sex: 1950-71, and Projections: 1975 and 1980.

Year of Graduation	High School			College		
	No. in thousands	Percent Male	Percent Female	No. in thousands	Percent Male	Percent Female
1950	1220	47.6	52.4	432	76.1	23.9
1958	1506	48.2	51.8	363	66.4	33.6
1960	1864	48.2	51.8	392	64.8	35.2
1962	1925	48.9	51.1	417	62.6	37.4
1964	2290	49.0	51.0	498	59.8	40.0
1965	2665	49.3	50.7	534	59.6	40.4
1966	2672	49.6	50.4	556	59.5	40.3
1967	2680	49.7	50.3	595	59.7	40.3
1968	2702	49.6	50.3	672	58.5	41.5
1969	2839	49.6	50.4	764	58.1	41.9
1970	2906	49.5	50.5	784	58.2	41.8
1971	3102	49.7	50.3	816	58.0	42.2
Estimates						
1975	3507	50.1	49.9	959	55.5	44.5
1980	3759	50.6	49.4	1133	53.7	46.3

Source: Adapted from *Statistical Abstracts of the U.S.* (Washington, D.C.: U.S. Department of Commerce, Bureau of the Census, 1972), table 159, p. 108.

Among men, in 1948, the proportion represented in the managerial and professional subcategories was 61 percent; in 1971, it was 70 percent. One can find little evidence in these statistics for a major shift in the occupational patterns of American women.

Two other measures of socioeconomic status that need to be commented upon in this context are education and income. As shown by the percentages in table 3-6, the proportion of women who have graduated from high school is roughly proportional to their representation in the population. The percentage of women who have completed four years of college is smaller than their representation in the population. Between 1950 and 1970 the proportion of women who have graduated from college has increased by 70 percent; but as the statistics for the beginning of this decade indicate, there are still almost six men for every four women who have completed four years of college.

The 1970 census compares selected occupational distributions among men and women by levels of education. The percentages in table 3-7, which summarize the relationships between sex levels of

Table 3-7

Educational Attainment for Males and Females Over Twenty-Five Years of Age in Six Occupational Categories[a] (1969)

Education	Males						Females					
	1	2	3	4	5	6	1	2	3	4	5	6
No Schooling	.1	.2	.3	.3	.6	1.0	.6	.3	.2	.4	.6	1.3
Elem.: 1-4 yrs.	.2	.7	.7	.7	2.5	4.3	1.7	.7	.2	.6	1.9	3.3
Elem.: 5-7 yrs.	.6	2.9	3.6	2.9	9.5	13.5	6.1	2.9	1.2	3.9	8.0	13.8
Elem.: 8 yrs.	1.1	5.3	6.7	5.3	13.5	16.1	8.8	5.8	3.3	9.2	13.4	17.9
H.S.: 1-3 yrs.	3.9	13.3	18.1	14.4	25.7	27.2	20.2	17.2	15.1	24.6	28.1	32.4
H.S.: 4 yrs.	16.2	32.1	41.9	35.0	38.0	31.7	39.5	42.5	59.5	46.9	38.1	28.5
College: 1-2 yrs.	12.8	15.8	15.4	17.8	7.0	4.4	9.3	14.0	14.7	9.4	6.5	2.1
College: 3 yrs.	4.3	3.9	3.0	4.3	1.0	.6	2.2	2.6	1.7	1.5	.9	.3
College: 4 yrs.	23.2	15.6	7.0	14.6	.6	.8	7.0	7.3	3.3	2.8	1.9	.3
College: 5 yrs.	11.6	4.1	1.6	2.4	.3	.2	2.3	2.6	.5	.4	.3	.1
College: 6+ yrs.	26.1	6.0	1.7	2.3	.3	.2	2.4	4.0	.4	.3	.3	.1
Total	100	100	100	100	100	100	100	100	100	100	100	100

a1. Professional, technical and kindred workers
2. Managers and Administrators
3. Clerical and kindred workers
4. Sales Workers
5. Craftsmen and Foremen
6. Operatives

Source: Adapted from *1970 U.S. Census of Population* (U.S. Department of Commerce, 1973), Subject Reports.

Table 3-8
Median Annual Income in Dollars by Type of Employment and by Sex and Percentage of Female Earnings to Male Earnings: 1956-69 (in Dollars)

Year	Professional and Technical			Managers and Officials		
	Male	Female	Ratio[a]	Male	Female	Ratio
1956	7,484	4,672	62.4	7,638	4,512	59.1
1957	7,410	4,713	63.6	7,558	4,812	63.7
1958	7,777	4,950	63.6	7,679	4,503	58.6
1959	8,161	5,236	64.2	8,251	4,697	56.9
1960	8,367	5,125	61.2	7,818	4,132	52.8
1961	8,685	5,670	65.3	8,114	3,967	48.9
1962	8,764	5,566	63.5	7,943	4,306	54.2
1963	9,073	5,658	62.4	8,337	4,282	51.4
1964	9,577	5,753	60.1	8,483	4,170	49.2
1965	9,330	6,082	65.2	8,708	4,635	53.2
1966	9,868	6,195	62.8	9,461	4,794	50.7
1967	10,193	6,590	64.6	9,691	5,182	53.5
1968	10,542	6,610	62.7	9,794	5,101	52.1
1969	11,151	6,935	62.2	10,453	5,549	53.1

[a]Ratio (×100) Earnings of Females to Males.
Source: Adapted from Abbot L. Ferris, *Indicators of Trends in the Status of American Women* (New York: Russell Sage Foundation, 1971).

education and occupations, show that a much smaller proportion of the women in the professional and managerial categories, as opposed to the men, have completed at least four years of college. For example, 61 percent of the men in the professional categories have at least four years of college, compared to 12 percent of the women in the same occupational category. Among men and women who are managers and administrators, 26 percent of the men, compared to 14 percent of the women, have completed at least four years of college. Of course, the categories "professional, technical, and kindred workers" and "managers and administrators" are such broad labels that they can place directors of the largest corporations and government agencies side by side with the managers of social work agencies, community libraries, or stenographic pools. But even with this caution, the fact that women with college and postcollege degrees are not overrepresented in the clerical, sales, and craft categories suggests that women with special skills (as represented by level of education) are no more likely to have to accept jobs that carry lower prestige than do men.

| | Clerical | | | Sales Workers | | | Operatives | |
Male	Female	Ratio[a]	Male	Female	Ratio[a]	Male	Female	Ratio[a]
5,617	4,026	71.7	6,406	2,675	41.8	5,421	3,369	62.1
5,646	4,066	72.0	6,362	2,831	44.5	5,439	3,230	59.4
5,778	4,045	70.0	6,366	2,786	43.8	5,325	3,278	61.6
6,125	4,171	68.1	6,621	2,794	42.2	5,501	3,482	63.3
6,222	4,204	67.6	6,870	2,809	40.9	5,876	3,492	59.4
6,228	4,325	69.4	7,002	2,781	39.7	5,989	3,432	57.3
6,455	4,400	68.2	7,159	2,998	41.9	6,135	3,629	59.2
6,662	4,469	67.1	7,426	2,758	37.1	6,297	3,539	56.2
6,930	4,540	65.5	7,755	3,052	39.4	6,394	3,640	56.9
6,927	4,658	67.2	7,970	3,232	40.6	6,378	3,610	56.6
7,013	4,626	66.0	8,097	3,287	40.6	6,577	3,631	55.2
7,037	4,688	66.6	8,080	3,380	41.8	6,576	3,783	57.5
7,324	4,778	65.2	8,292	3,388	40.8	6,773	3,956	58.4
7,537	4,898	65.0	8,762	3,519	40.2	6,950	4,082	58.7

Perhaps the measure that offers the best evidence that women do face discrimination in the market place is income. By controlling on types of occupations, as shown in table 3-8, or on levels of education, as shown in table 3-9, and then comparing annual incomes between men and women, we find that women consistently receive lower salaries than men. For example, between 1956 and 1969, women in the same occupational category received as low as 37 percent of the annual salary of their male coworkers. There is no indication on the basis of the data from 1956 to 1969 that the gap is narrowing between men's and women's incomes in the same, admittedly broad occupational categories.

Indeed, when educational levels and occupational categories are not held constant, as shown in table 3-10, then the annual earning of white women between 1956 and 1968 are shown to have decreased in comparison to those of white men. Only the earnings of nonwhite women have increased when compared with those of nonwhite men during this period.

The picture that emerges from these statistics about the current status of the American woman is not radically different from the picture that could have been drawn one or even two decades earlier.

Table 3-9

Median Annual Income in Dollars of Full-Time Employees Over Fourteen Years of Age by Education and Sex: 1969

Education	Male	Female
None	5,029	3,179
Elem.: 1-4 yrs.	4,987	3,031
Elem.: 5-7 yrs.	6,308	3,388
Elem.: 8 yrs.	7,295	3,786
H.S.: 1-3 yrs.	8,102	4,076
H.S.: 4 yrs.	8,952	4,945
College: 1-2 yrs.	9,929	5,619
College: 3 yrs.	10,851	6,273
College: 4 yrs.	12,856	7,181
College: 5 yrs.	12,707	8,483
College: 6+ yrs.	14,710	9,218
All Categories	8,845	4,794

Source: Adapted from *1970 U.S. Census of Population* (Washington, D.C.: U.S. Department of Commerce, 1973), Subject Reports.

More of them are delaying marriage by a few years; more of them are going on to and completing four years of college; more of them are having fewer children; and more of them are working outside their homes once their children have entered elementary school. These facts summarize the major demographic changes that have occurred in women's status in American society. Perhaps more significant, however, has been the absence of big changes in such areas as the types of jobs women occupied in 1970 compared with those they occupied in 1960 and in 1950; and in the amounts of money they earned compared with that of men in 1970 as opposed to 1960 or 1950.

The primary objectives and goals of the contemporary women's movement is not to get women out of the homes and into the factories and offices. These were the goals of the women's movement of the 1920s. Today, the emphasis and the disputes focus on equal opportunities vis-à-vis men for positions and jobs that carry prestige, authority, and appropriate monetary compensation. Success is measured by the proportion of women in managerial and professional positions, by the proportion of women who have completed college and university, and by the absence of lower salary scales for women in the same types of jobs as men. On these issues tnere is no evidence that big changes have already occurred. This is

Table 3-10

Median Annual Income of Year-Round, Full-Time Civilian Workers and Ratio of Female Earnings to Male Earnings, by Race: 1956-70

| | Median Annual Income in Dollars | | | | | | Ratio (× 100) of Earnings of Females to Earnings of Males | | |
| | All Races | | White | | Nonwhite | | | | |
Year	Male	Female	Male	Female	Male	Female	All Races	White	Nonwhite
1956	5,716	3,619	6,029	3,786	3,727	2,095	63.3	62.8	56.2
1957	5,830	3,721	6,123	3,843	3,880	2,308	63.8	62.8	59.5
1958	5,932	3,735	6,244	3,883	4,055	2,394	63.0	62.2	59.0
1959	6,220	3,812	6,514	3,947	3,987	2,622	61.3	60.6	65.8
1960	6,313	3,830	6,659	4,010	4,456	2,789	60.7	60.2	62.6
1961	6,507	3,855	6,838	4,047	4,516	2,704	59.2	59.2	59.9
1962	6,617	3,924	6,929	4,141	4,369	2,620	59.3	59.8	60.0
1963	6,793	4,004	7,131	4,229	4,662	2,690	58.9	59.3	57.7
1964	6,954	4,113	7,283	4,326	4,803	2,998	59.1	59.4	62.4
1965	7,046	4,222	7,395	4,402	4,718	3,106	59.9	59.5	65.8
1966	7,350	4,230	7,680	4,451	4,854	3,161	57.6	58.0	65.1
1967	7,484	4,324	7,828	4,579	5,282	3,504	57.8	58.5	66.3
1968	7,664	4,457	8,014	4,700	5,603	3,677	58.2	58.6	65.6
1970	8,845	4,794					54.2		

Source: Adapted from Abbott L. Ferris, *Indicators of Trends in the Status of American Women* (New York: Russell Sage Foundation, 1971), Statistics: 1956-1968. *1972 Statistical Abstract of the U.S* (Washington, D.C.: U.S. Department of Commerce, Bureau of the Census, 1972), table 368, p. 231, Statistics: 1970.

not to say that the women's movement has not accomplished anything of significance. Legal rights and changes in consciousness and
self-image are important in and of themselves; and there have been
changes in these areas.

4

Arrest Statistics

Chapter 4 begins the second major section of this volume. It examines statistics concerning the proportion of women as opposed to men who have been arrested for different types of crimes over the past two decades.

Longitudinal, national data about the number of women involved in crime and the types of crimes for which they are charged have been available since 1930, when the Federal Bureau of Investigation published its first *Uniform Crime Report*. These reports, currently based on data obtained from approximately 10,000 law enforcement agencies all over the country, describe the number of arrests in a given year, the offenses for which suspects have been arrested, and the age, sex, and racial backgrounds of those arrested. Arrest rates and trends are shown by cities, suburbs, and rural areas, as well as for the United States as a whole.

The FBI divides specific crimes for which arrest data are available into two categories. Type I offenses include: (1) criminal homicide, including murder and non-negligent manslaughter and manslaughter by negligence; (2) forcible rape; (3) robbery; (4) aggravated assault; (5) burglary; (6) larceny; and (7) auto theft. These offenses are used to establish an "Index in the Uniform Crime Reporting Program" to measure the trend and distribution of crime in the United States. These particular offenses are selected because as a group "they represent the most common local crime problem. They are all serious crimes either by their nature or due to the volume in which they occur" [*Uniform Crime Report* 1972, p. 1].

Type II offenses include: (8) other assaults; (9) arson; (10) forgery and counterfeiting; (11) fraud; (12) embezzlement; (13) stolen property, buying, receiving, possessing; (14) vandalism; (15) weapons (carrying, possessing, etc.); (16) prostitution and commercialized vice; (17) sex offenses (except forcible rape, prostitution, and commercialized vice); (18) narcotic drug laws; (19) gambling; (20) offenses against the family and children; (21) driving under the influence; (22) liquor laws; (23) drunkenness;

33

(24) disorderly conduct; (25) vagrancy; (26) all other offenses; and (27) suspicion.

This chapter reports primarily on Type I offenses; they are the most serious and the most common. Rape will not be included, because it is almost exclusively a male offense. Some of the Type II offenses are commented upon, usually because there has been a change in the arrest pattern for women or because they are offenses for which arrest rates for women are consistently high.

As this chapter unfolds, it may appear that we are using arrest statistics as proxies for describing crime rates among men and women without regard for the hazards of doing so. We wish to emphasize at this time that we are aware of the dangers of using the terms *arrests* and *crimes committed* interchangeably, and that arrest statistics may not be the most reliable source of data for determining actual crime rates. But, unfortunately, there are no other data prior to these statistics that provide information about the characteristics of the suspect as well as the offense he or she is believed to have committed.

Criminologists usually prefer to use statistics computed on the basis of crimes known to the police for determining crime rates, but unfortunately those statistics do not identify the suspect in any way. We use arrest data in this volume to describe female crime rates and to compare rates between men and women for different types of offenses because they are the only data available. We also recognize that the proportions of arrest vary considerably from one type of offense to another. For example, the proportion of crimes in the Type I category that were cleared by arrest in 1972 are: murder, 82 percent; forcible rape, 57 percent; aggravated assault, 60 percent; robbery, 30 percent; burglary, 19 percent; larceny, 20 percent; and auto theft, 17 percent. Arrest rates are obviously more accurate proxies for behavior in violent types of crimes than they are for crimes against property.

With these qualifications and precautions in mind, we turn to the arrest data and report first the proportion of women who have been arrested for all types of crime as well as for those crimes that are included in the Crime Index from 1953 to 1972. Table 4-1 also describes the average rate of change in the proportion of women arrested in both categories for the following time periods: 1953-1972, 1958-1972, and 1967 and 1972. The last period is particularly crucial,

Table 4-1
Percentage of Females Among Arrests: 1953-72[a]

Year	All Crimes	Serious Crimes[b]
1953	10.84	9.40
1954	10.97	8.89
1955	11.00	9.12
1956	10.91	9.06
1957	10.63	9.29
1958	10.61	9.73
1959	10.68	10.54
1960	11.04	10.95
1961	11.26	11.47
1962	11.47	12.38
1963	11.68	12.65
1964	11.93	13.54
1965	12.12	14.37
1966	12.33	14.80
1967	12.67	15.03
1968	13.08	15.04
1969	13.82	16.58
1970	14.58	18.04
1971	15.07	18.34
1972	15.27	19.25
Average Rate of Change 1953-72	+0.23 percent per year	+0.52 percent per year
Average Rate of Change 1958-72	+0.33	+0.68
Average Rate of Change 1967-72	+0.52	+0.84

[a]From *Uniform Crime Reports*. Arrest Data for cities with populations 2500 and above; 1953 was the first year these data were reported.

[b]Serious crimes are all those included in the Crime Index except rape.

Source: Adapted from *Uniform Crime Reports* (Washington, D.C.: Federal Bureau of Investigation, U.S. Department of Justice, 1953-1972).

because our expectation is that the rate of change would be marked by the greatest increase during this period.

Table 4-1 shows that in 1972, one out of every 6.5 persons arrested was a woman. The average rate of change over the entire two decades was .23. For the serious crimes, in 1953 one out of 10.6 persons arrested was a woman. In 1972, the proportion had dropped to one out of 5.2. The average rate of increase was .52 for the entire period. The average increase in the proportion of women arrested for serious crimes is greater than the average increase in the proportion of women arrested for all crimes. Table 4-1 also shows that the average rate of increase was greatest in the period from 1967 to 1972: .52 for all crimes, and .84 for serious offenses. Note also that from 1961 onward the percentage of women arrested for serious crimes was greater than the percentage of women arrested for all offenses.

Table 4-2 reports the proportions of female and male arrests for serious crimes as a percentage of total male and female arrests for all crimes. In 1953, one out of 12.8 women arrested was for serious crimes as opposed to slightly less than one out of 10.9 men arrested. But two decades later, a higher proportion of women were arrested for serious offenses (about one out of four) than were men (about one out of five). The average rate of change among the women was greater during each of the three time periods than it was for the men. But the time span from 1967 to 1972 does not show a greater increase than do the time periods that extend farther back.

Table 4-3 describes the proportion of women arrested for those crimes of violence and property that are included in the index of serious offenses: homicide, robbery, aggravated assault; and burglary, larceny amounting to fifty dollars or more, and auto theft.

Table 4-3 disputes a popular impression that in recent years women have been committing crimes of violence at a much higher rate than they have in the past. In fact, the increase in the proportion of female arrests for serious crimes is owing almost wholly to the fact women seem to be committing more *property* offenses than they have in the past. Indeed, the percentage of women arrested for crimes of violence shows neither an upward nor a downward trend. Between 1953 and 1972, the percentages fluctuated from a high point of 13.51 in 1956 to a low of 10.33 in 1968. But the picture for property offenses is markedly different. In 1953, about one out of every twelve arrests was a woman. In 1972, one out of 4.7 persons arrested was a woman. Not only has there been a consistent increase since 1953 in the percentage of women who have been arrested for property offenses; the biggest increases have occurred in the period beginning in 1967. This last finding is most congruent with our major hypothesis, that women's participation in selective crimes will increase as her employment opportunities expand, as her interests, desires, and definitions of self shift from a more traditional to a more

Table 4-2
Males and Females Arrested for Serious Crimes as Percentages of
Their Respective Sex Cohorts Arrested for All Crimes: 1953-72

Year (1)	Females Arrested for Serious Crimes as Percent of All Females Arrested (2)	Males Arrested for Serious Crimes as Percent of All Males Arrested (3)	Difference Col. 2 − Col. 3
1953	7.8	9.2	−1.4
1954	8.2	10.3	−2.1
1955	8.5	10.4	−1.9
1956	8.2	10.3	−2.1
1957	9.3	10.8	−1.5
1958	9.9	10.9	−1.0
1959	10.6	10.8	−0.2
1960	12.4	12.6	−0.2
1961	13.4	13.2	+0.2
1962	14.6	13.3	+1.3
1963	15.9	14.4	+1.5
1964	18.0	15.6	+2.4
1965	18.9	15.5	+3.4
1966	20.1	16.1	+4.0
1967	20.8	16.9	+3.9
1968	20.7	17.8	+2.9
1969	22.2	17.9	+4.3
1970	23.8	18.4	+5.4
1971	24.2	19.2	+5.0
1972	25.2	19.2	+6.0
Average Rate of Change 1953-72	+0.92 percent per year	+0.53 percent per year	
Average Rate of Change 1958-72	+1.1	+0.59	
Average Rate of Change 1967-72	+0.90	+0.46	

Source: Adapted from *Uniform Crime Reports* (Washington, D.C.: Federal Bureau of Investigation, U.S. Department of Justice, 1953-1972).

"liberated" view. The crimes that are considered most salient for this hypothesis are various types of property, financial, and white-collar offenses.

Table 4-4 demonstrates the same phenomenon by its comparison of the proportions of men and women who have been arrested for the serious violent and property offenses among all the men and women

Table 4-3

Breakdown of Serious Crimes: Percentage of Females Arrested among All Arrests for Violent and Property Crimes: 1953-72

Year	Violent Crimes	Property Crimes	Serious Crimes
1953	11.93	8.46	9.40
1954	11.60	8.18	8.89
1955	12.03	8.36	9.12
1956	13.51	8.04	9.06
1957	13.06	8.51	9.29
1958	11.96	9.26	9.73
1959	12.73	10.07	10.54
1960	11.77	10.76	10.95
1961	11.61	11.44	11.47
1962	11.51	12.57	12.38
1963	11.56	12.87	12.65
1964	11.64	13.92	13.54
1965	11.41	14.99	14.37
1966	11.32	15.58	14.80
1967	10.79	16.00	15.03
1968	10.33	16.11	15.04
1969	10.63	17.96	16.58
1970	10.50	19.71	18.04
1971	10.91	20.06	18.34
1972	11.01	21.35	19.25
Average Rate of Change 1953-72	−0.05	+0.68	+0.52
Average Rate of Change 1958-72	−0.07	+0.86	+0.68
Average Rate of Change 1967-72	+0.04	+1.07	+0.84

Source: Adapted from *Uniform Crime Reports* (Washington, D.C.: Federal Bureau of Investigation, U.S. Department of Justice, 1953-1972).

who were arrested between 1953 and 1972. The proportion of men who have been arrested for violent offenses over the two decades has increased almost four times as much as has the proportion of women. For property offenses, it is the proportion of women who have been arrested that has increased threefold compared to the men.

Table 4-5 provides more details about the types of serious property and violent offenses for which women have been arrested. Note that among all six offenses, only one shows a marked increase over time. From 1960 on, the proportion of women who have been

Table 4-4
Females and Males Arrested for Crimes of Violence and Property as Percentage of All Arrests in Their Respective Sex Cohorts: 1953-72

Year	Violent Crimes		Property Crimes	
	Female	Male	Female	Male
1953	2.2	2.0	5.6	7.2
1954	2.2	2.1	6.0	8.2
1955	2.3	2.1	6.2	8.3
1956	2.3	1.9	5.9	8.4
1957	2.2	1.8	7.1	9.0
1958	2.1	1.9	7.8	9.0
1959	2.3	1.9	8.3	8.9
1960	2.5	2.4	9.9	10.2
1961	2.5	2.4	10.9	10.8
1962	2.4	2.4	12.2	10.9
1963	2.5	2.4	13.4	12.0
1964	2.6	2.6	15.4	13.0
1965	2.6	2.7	16.3	12.8
1966	2.8	3.0	17.3	13.1
1967	2.8	3.2	18.0	13.7
1968	2.5	3.5	18.2	14.3
1969	2.6	3.6	19.6	14.3
1970	2.5	3.6	21.3	14.8
1971	2.7	3.2	21.5	15.3
1972	2.9	4.4	22.3	14.8
Average Rate of Change 1953-72	+0.04	+0.03	+0.88	+0.40
Average Rate of Change 1958-72	+0.06	+0.18	+1.04	+0.41
Average Rate of Change 1967-72	+0.02	+0.24	+0.86	+0.22

Source: Adapted from *Uniform Crime Reports* (Washington, D.C.: Federal Bureau of Investigation, U.S. Department of Justice, 1953-1972).

charged with larceny or theft is much greater than are the proportions in any of the other offenses, property as well as violent. It is interesting that until about 1960 the proportions of women arrested for homicide and aggravated assault were very similar to those arrested for larceny, but since 1960, the percentage in the latter category has almost doubled, whereas the proportions have remained roughly the same for the former offenses.

Table 4-6 compares the proportion of males and females arrested for those same Type I offenses shown in table 4-5, out of the total cohort of males and females arrested for all crimes. These data show

Table 4-5
Females Arrested as Percentage of All Arrests for Type I Offenses: 1953-72[a]

Year	Criminal Homicide	Robbery	Aggravated Assault	Burglary	Larceny-Theft	Auto Theft
1953	14.1	4.3	15.9	2.0	13.9	2.6
1954	14.2	4.2	15.9	2.2	13.0	2.5
1955	14.2	4.2	16.0	2.3	13.3	2.6
1956	14.8	4.3	17.6	2.3	12.6	2.5
1957	14.7	3.9	17.5	2.0	13.2	2.7
1958	16.4	4.5	15.7	2.4	14.3	3.2
1959	16.8	4.6	16.4	2.7	15.4	3.2
1960	16.1	4.6	15.3	2.8	16.8	3.6
1961	15.9	4.9	15.2	3.2	18.0	3.7
1962	17.2	5.1	14.7	3.6	19.6	3.9
1963	15.9	4.9	14.9	3.3	20.1	3.7
1964	16.6	5.3	14.4	3.7	21.4	4.3
1965	16.3	5.3	14.4	3.8	23.2	4.2
1966	15.9	5.1	14.0	3.8	24.0	4.1
1967	15.4	5.2	13.6	4.1	24.8	4.3
1968	15.4	5.5	13.1	4.1	25.2	4.9
1969	14.8	6.3	13.2	4.3	27.2	5.1
1970	14.8	6.2	13.3	4.6	29.0	5.0
1971	16.0	6.4	13.9	4.8	29.1	6.0
1972	15.6	6.6	13.9	5.1	30.8	5.7
Average Rate of Change 1953-72	+0.08	+0.12	−0.10	+0.16	+0.89	+0.16
Average Rate of Change 1958-72	−0.06	+0.14	−0.13	+0.19	+1.18	+0.18
Average Rate of Change 1967-72	+0.04	+0.28	+0.06	+0.20	+1.20	+0.28

[a]Rape has been omitted.

Source: Adapted from *Uniform Crime Reports* (Washington, D.C.: Federal Bureau of Investigation, U.S. Dept. of Justice, 1953-1972).

Table 4-6
Serious Crimes: Females and Males Arrested as Percentage of Total Arrests in Their Respective Sex Cohorts: 1953-72

Year	Criminal Homicide		Robbery		Aggravated Assault		Burglary		Larceny-Theft		Auto Theft	
	Female	Male	Female	Male	Female	Male	Female	Male	Female	Male	Female	Male
1953	0.2	0.2	0.3	0.7	1.7	1.1	0.4	2.3	4.9	3.7	0.3	1.2
1954	0.2	0.2	0.3	0.8	1.7	1.1	0.5	2.6	5.2	4.3	0.3	1.3
1955	0.2	0.2	0.3	0.7	1.8	1.2	0.5	2.6	5.4	4.3	0.3	1.4
1956	0.3	0.2	0.2	0.6	1.8	1.1	0.5	2.5	5.1	4.4	0.3	1.5
1957	0.2	0.2	0.2	0.6	1.8	1.0	0.5	2.7	6.2	4.8	0.4	1.5
1958	0.2	0.2	0.3	0.7	1.6	1.0	0.6	2.8	6.8	4.8	0.4	1.4
1959	0.2	0.2	0.3	0.6	1.8	1.1	0.6	2.7	7.3	4.8	0.4	1.4
1960	0.2	0.1	0.3	0.9	2.0	1.4	0.8	3.3	8.6	5.3	0.5	1.6
1961	0.2	0.1	0.4	0.9	1.9	1.4	0.9	3.6	9.5	5.5	0.5	1.7
1962	0.2	0.1	0.4	0.9	1.8	1.4	1.0	3.5	10.6	5.6	0.6	1.8
1963	0.2	0.1	0.4	0.9	1.9	1.4	1.0	3.8	11.8	6.2	0.6	2.0
1964	0.2	0.1	0.4	0.9	2.0	1.6	1.1	4.0	13.6	6.8	0.7	2.2
1965	0.2	0.1	0.4	1.0	2.0	1.6	1.1	4.0	14.5	6.6	0.7	2.2
1966	0.2	0.1	0.4	1.0	2.2	1.9	1.1	4.0	15.5	6.9	0.7	2.2
1967	0.2	0.1	0.5	1.2	2.1	1.9	1.3	4.4	16.0	7.0	0.7	2.3
1968	0.2	0.2	0.5	1.4	1.8	1.9	1.3	4.7	16.1	7.2	0.8	2.4
1969	0.2	0.2	0.6	1.5	1.8	1.9	1.3	4.5	17.5	7.5	0.8	2.3
1970	0.2	0.2	0.6	1.5	1.7	1.9	1.3	4.6	19.3	8.1	0.7	2.1
1971	0.2	0.2	0.7	1.7	1.8	2.0	1.4	4.8	19.4	8.4	0.7	2.1
1972	0.2	0.2	0.7	1.8	2.0	2.2	1.4	4.7	20.2	8.2	0.7	1.9
Average Rate of Change 1953-72	0	0	+0.02	+0.06	+0.02	+0.06	+0.05	+0.13	+0.81	+0.24	+0.02	+0.04
Average Rate of Change 1958-72	0	0	+0.03	+0.08	+0.03	+0.09	+0.06	+0.14	+0.96	+0.24	+0.02	+0.04
Average Rate of Change 1967-72	0	+0.02	+0.04	+0.12	-0.02	+0.06	+0.02	0	+0.84	+0.24	0	-0.08

Source: Adapted from *Uniform Crime Reports* (Washington, D.C.: Federal Bureau of Investigation, U.S. Dept. of Justice, 1953-1972).

that within each of the violent crime categories, the differences in arrest rates between men and women are either nonexistent or slight. For criminal homicide the percentage of males and females has remained remarkably stable over the last twenty years, and the average rate of change is practically nil. For the crimes of robbery and aggravated assault, males register a steady increase over females. Even within the last five years, there has been no significant increase in the proportion of females who have been arrested for these crimes in contrast to all other offenses.

The most striking change is in the arrests for larceny. The average rate of increase during any of the time spans within the two decades shows that rates for women have increased between three and four times as much as they have for men. In 1953, about one out of every twenty women arrested was for larceny. In 1972, the ratio was down to one out of five. For males the proportion shifted from one out of 27 to one out of 12.2. Burglary and auto theft were as much male-dominated offenses in 1972 as they were in 1953. Burglary, perhaps more than any of the other offenses examined thus far, involves skills that are usually acquired within a criminal subculture. Women have not been connected into such networks; their opportunities for acquiring such skills are therefore much more limited.

Tables 4-7 and 4-8 describe trends in the proportion of female arrests for selective offenses in the Type II category. The figures show that in 1972 approximately one out of four persons arrested for forgery was a woman, and one out of three and a half arrests for embezzlement and fraud involved a woman. On the one hand, then, if present trends in these crimes persist, approximately equal numbers of men and women will be arrested for larceny and for fraud and embezzlement by the 1990s; and for forgery and counterfeiting the proportions should be equal by the 2010s. On the other hand, if trends from 1958 to 1972 continue, women have been and will be accounting for a lesser share of criminal homicide and aggravated assault arrests.

Table 4-9 ranks the proportion of men and women who were arrested in 1972 for the ten most frequently cited Type I and Type II offenses and indicates the average rate of change between 1958 and 1972. These ten offenses account for 71 percent of all men and 63 percent of all women arrested in 1972.

Among the women, there has been a big change in two categories: larceny, which has increased sharply, and drunkenness,

Table 4-7
Other Crimes: Females Arrested as Percentage of All People Arrested for Various Crimes: 1953-72

Year	Embezzlement and Fraud	Forgery and Counterfeiting	Offenses Against Family and Children	Narcotic Drug Laws	Prostitution and Commercialized Vice
1953	18.3	14.0	9.3	15.7	73.1
1954	14.4	13.4	9.6	17.5	70.1
1955	15.6	15.2	9.8	17.1	68.8
1956	15.5	16.6	9.1	16.3	62.9
1957	14.4	14.8	9.0	15.6	69.2
1958	14.3	15.1	8.6	16.4	69.0
1959	14.9	16.2	8.9	16.2	65.2
1960	15.7	16.8	9.7	14.6	73.5
1961	15.7	17.5	11.2	15.4	71.8
1962	17.6	18.1	11.0	15.1	76.1
1963	18.3	18.7	11.5	14.2	77.0
1964	19.5	19.3	11.3	14.1	81.2
1965	20.7	19.2	11.0	13.4	77.6
1966	21.8	20.9	12.1	13.8	79.3
1967	23.4	21.4	11.4	13.7	77.2
1968	24.4	22.3	10.9	15.0	78.0
1969	26.3	23.2	11.4	15.5	79.5
1970	27.8	24.4	11.3	15.7	79.1
1971	27.4	24.8	11.6	16.3	77.4
1972	29.7	25.4	12.3	15.7	73.5
Average Rate of Change 1953-72	+0.60	+0.60	+0.16	0	+0.02
Average Rate of Change 1958-72	+1.10	+0.74	+0.26	-0.05	+0.32
Average Rate of Change 1967-72	+1.26	+0.80	+0.18	+0.40	-0.74

Source: Adapted from *Uniform Crime Reports* (Washington, D.C.: Federal Bureau of Investigation, U.S. Dept. of Justice, 1953-1972).

44

Table 4-8
Other Crimes: Females and Males Arrested for Various Crimes as Percentage of Total Arrests in Their Respective Sex Cohorts: 1953-72

Year	Embezzlement and Fraud		Forgery and Counterfeiting		Offenses Against Family and Children		Narcotic Drug Laws		Prostitution and Commercialized Vice	
	Female	Male	Female	Male	Female	Male	Female	Male	Female	Male
1953	1.1	0.6	0.5	0.4	0.9	1.1	0.5	0.3	7.7	0.3
1954	1.0	0.8	0.6	0.5	1.1	1.3	0.6	0.4	8.6	0.5
1955	1.0	0.7	0.6	0.4	1.1	1.3	0.6	0.3	8.3	0.5
1956	0.9	0.6	0.7	0.4	0.9	1.1	0.5	0.3	4.1	0.3
1957	1.1	0.7	0.6	0.4	0.9	1.1	0.5	0.3	4.0	0.2
1958	1.1	0.8	0.7	0.5	0.8	1.0	0.6	0.4	4.9	0.3
1959	1.1	0.8	0.7	0.4	0.8	1.0	0.6	0.4	4.3	0.3
1960	1.3	0.8	0.8	0.5	0.8	0.9	0.8	0.6	4.7	0.2
1961	1.3	0.8	0.9	0.5	0.9	0.9	0.9	0.6	4.4	0.2
1962	1.3	0.8	0.9	0.5	0.9	0.9	0.9	0.7	4.3	0.2
1963	1.5	0.9	0.9	0.5	1.0	1.0	0.8	0.7	4.2	0.2
1964	1.6	0.8	0.9	0.5	0.9	1.0	1.0	0.8	4.3	0.2
1965	1.6	0.8	0.8	0.5	0.8	0.9	1.1	1.0	4.7	0.2
1966	1.6	0.9	0.9	0.5	0.9	0.9	1.4	1.2	4.8	0.2
1967	1.7	0.9	0.9	0.5	0.7	0.8	2.0	1.8	4.9	0.2
1968	1.7	0.8	0.9	0.5	0.6	0.7	3.3	2.8	4.9	0.2
1969	1.8	0.9	1.0	0.5	0.6	0.7	4.4	3.8	5.0	0.2
1970	2.0	0.9	1.0	0.5	0.5	0.7	5.6	5.1	4.5	0.2
1971	2.3	1.0	1.0	0.5	0.4	0.6	5.9	5.4	4.4	0.2
1972	2.4	1.0	1.0	0.5	0.4	0.5	6.0	5.8	3.4	0.2
Average Rate of Change 1953-72	+0.07	+0.02	+0.03	+0.01	−0.03	−0.03	+0.28	+0.28	−0.23	−0.01
Average Rate of Change 1958-72	+0.09	+0.01	+0.02	0	−0.03	−0.04	+0.40	+0.40	−0.11	−0.01
Average Rate of Change 1967-72	+0.14	+0.02	+0.02	0	−0.06	−0.06	+0.80	+0.80	−0.30	0

Source: Adapted from *Uniform Crime Reports* (Washington, D.C.: Federal Bureau of Investigation, U.S. Dept. of Justice, 1953-1972).

Table 4-9
Rank Order of Offenses for which Females and Males Are Most Likely to Be Arrested—1972

Rank	Offense	Percent Arrested out of All Female Arrests	Average Rate of Change, 1958-72 (percent/yr.)	Offense	Percent Arrested out of All Male Arrests	Average Rate of Change, 1958-72 (percent/yr.)
1	Larceny-Theft	20.2	+0.96	Drunkenness	22.9	−1.24
2	Drunkenness	9.8	−1.25	Drunken Driving	9.0	+0.31
3	Disorderly Conduct	8.5	−0.60	Disorderly Conduct	9.0	−0.60
4	Narcotic Drug Laws	6.0	+0.40	Larceny-Theft	8.2	+0.24
5	Other Assaults	4.1	+0.06	Narcotic Drug Laws	5.8	+0.40
6	Drunken Driving	3.8	+0.11	Burglary	4.7	+0.14
7	Prostitution	3.4	−0.11	Other Assaults	4.5	+0.09
8	Liquor Laws	2.7	−0.04	Liquor Laws	2.9	−0.06
9	Embezzlement and Fraud	2.4	+0.10	Aggravated Assault	2.2	+0.09
10	Aggravated Assault	2.0	+0.03	Robbery	1.8	+0.06

Source: Adapted from *Uniform Crime Reports* (Washington, D.C.: Federal Bureau of Investigation, U.S. Dept. of Justice, 1953-1972).

which has decreased sharply. Disorderly conduct has declined by about half as much as the first two offenses, and narcotics has increased. For all the other offenses, the pattern has remained stable from 1958 onwards. Among men, the ordering has been even more stable. Except for a decline in the proportion arrested for drunkenness and disorderly conduct and an increase in arrests for narcotics, there has been no marked changes. Among both men and women the sharp decrease in arrests for drunkenness and disorderly conduct may be as much, or even more, an indication of a shift in police behavior than in the behavior of the men and women arrested.

In sum, the arrest data tell us the following about women's participation in crime: the proportion of female arrests in 1972 was greater than the proportion arrested one or two decades earlier; the increase was greater for serious offenses than it was for all Type I and Type II offenses combined. The increase in female arrest rates among the serious offenses was owing almost entirely to women's greater participation in property offenses, especially larceny. In 1953, roughly one out of seven arrests for larceny involved a woman; in 1972, the proportion was approximately one out of three. Contrary to impressions that might be gleaned from the mass media, the proportion of female arrests for violent crimes has changed hardly at all over the past two decades. Female arrest rates for homicide, for example, has been the most stable of all violent offenses. Further probing of female arrest rates in the Type II offenses revealed that the offenses that showed the greatest increases were embezzlement and fraud, and forgery and counterfeiting. The increases were especially marked for the period from 1967 to 1972. None of the other offenses included in either Type I or Type II, save larceny/theft, showed as big a shift as did these two white-collar offenses. Should the average rate of change that occurred between 1967 and 1972 continue, female arrest rates for larceny/theft, embezzlement, and fraud will be commensurate to women's representation in the society or, in other words, roughly equal to male arrest rates. There are no other offenses among those contained in the *Uniform Crime Reports*, save prostitution, in which females are so highly represented.

One final word of caution about interpreting the statistics reported in this chapter. These statistics describe arrests, not known or observed behavior at the scene of a crime. From the arrests, we infer actual participation in the criminal act. But in discussing women and crime, this inference might be especially fanciful, because of the discretion available to police and the way in which the police have been presumed to exercise that discretion.

Remember Pollak's argument that the differential rate of crime attributed to men and women was owing in large measure to chivalry on the part of law enforcement officials. Indeed, Pollak and other authors might claim that the sharp increase in the percent of women who have been arrested in the last half dozen years is because the police have become less chivalrous or less paternalistic, and that they are treating women as they would male suspects. Indeed, in large measure perhaps, the phenomena we are witnessing are changes in the attitudes and behavior of the police rather than in the propensities of women to engage in crime. The fact, however, that the rates of female arrests have varied by the nature of the offense indicates that the hypothesized change in police behavior cannot account for all of the shifts. There would be no reason to assume, for example, that police would respond to female property offenders differently than they would to women who were suspected of killing or assaulting their victims.

Two final observations: one, it is plausible to assume that the police are becoming less "chivalrous" to women suspects and that women are beginning to receive more "equal" treatment; two, police behavior alone cannot account for the large increases in larceny, fraud, embezzlement, and forgery by women that have occurred over the last half dozen years, and the absence of increases in homicide, aggravated assaults, and other violent crimes.

The other explanation is that women are committing those types of crimes that their participation in the labor force provide them with greater opportunities to commit than they have had in the past. This explanation also assumes that women have no greater store of morality than do men. Their propensities to commit crimes do not differ, but in the past their opportunities have been much more limited. As women's opportunities to commit crimes increase, so will their criminal behavior; and the types of crimes they commit will resemble much more closely those committed by men.

5 Women in Court

Two schools of thought prevail on how women defendants are treated at the bar of justice. Most observers feel that women receive preferential treatment, which in operational terms means that they are less likely to be convicted than men for the same type of offense; if convicted, they are less likely to be sentenced; and if sentenced, they are likely to receive milder sentences. The factors that are thought to motivate judges toward leniency vis-à-vis women are chivalry, naïvete (for example, judges often say that they cannot help but compare women defendants with other women they know well; namely, their mothers and wives whom they cannot imagine behaving in the manner attributed to the defendant), and practicality. Most of the women defendants have young children, and sending them to prison places too much of a burden on the rest of the society.

A particular manifestation of the preferential treatment toward women that many attribute to trial court judges takes the form of paternalism. Nagel and Weitzman (1971) assert that paternalistic behavior has favorable as well as unfavorable consequences for women defendants. The favorable consequences are that women are less likely to remain in custody during the pretrial period than are men. Once tried, they are less likely to be convicted; and if convicted, they are likely to receive milder sentences. The unfavorable consequences are that women are less likely to have an attorney, a preliminary hearing, or a jury trial.

Using data originally collected by Silverstein in a national survey of the defense of the poor, Nagel and Weitzman compared the treatment that men and women charged with assault and larceny received in the trial courts [Silverstein 1965]. Their results are shown in table 5-1.

On the basis of these data, Nagel and Weitzman concluded that paternalism prevails almost equally for both types of offenses, save that women are more likely to be jailed in assault than in larceny cases. They attribute the closer treatment of men and women in

Table 5-1
How the Treatment of Females Differs from Males as Defendants in Criminal Cases[a]

Case Type and Treatment Stage	Number of Defendants With Available Info.		Percent Receiving the Treatment		Difference in percentage points	Does paternalism hypothesis seem to be confirmed?
	Females	Males	Females	Males		
I. GRAND LARCENY CASES						
A. Being Jailed						
1. Released on bail	63	771	76	50	26	Yes
2. Had less than 2 months delay of those awaiting trial in jail	10	231	60	67	X	Too few women not released on bail
3. Case dismissed or acquitted	71	841	24	13	11	Yes
4. Received suspended sentence or probation of those convicted	47	656	64	43	21	Yes
5. Received less than one year imprisonment of those imprisoned	9	241	33	45	X	Too few women
B. Formal Safeguards						
6. Received preliminary hearing	42	606	57	55	2	Difference too small
7. Had or given a lawyer	61	781	90	87	3	Difference too small
8. Received a jury trial of those tried	18	283	47	31	X	Too few women

II. FELONIOUS ASSAULT CASES

A. Being Jailed						
1. Released on bail	43	615	77	58	19	Yes
2. Had less than 2 months delay of those awaiting trial in jail	6	152	17	49	X	Too few women released on bail
3. Case dismissed or acquitted	45	638	36	23	13	Yes
4. Received suspended sentence or probation of those convicted	25	415	44	36	8	Yes
5. Received less than one year imprisonment of those imprisoned	9	172	89	57	X	Too few women imprisoned
B. Formal Safeguards						
6. Received preliminary hearing	31	451	74	73	1	Difference too small
7. Had or given a lawyer	42	620	88	89	1	Difference too small
8. Received a jury trial of those tried	24	262	19	45	26	Yes

[a]Based on 1103 grand larceny cases and 846 felonious assault cases from all 50 states for 1962.

Source: Adapted from S. Nagel and L. Weitzman, "Women as Litigants," Hastings Law Journal, 23 (Nov. 1971) 171-198.

assault cases to the fact that assault is a more manly type of crime and women who commit it pay the price for their behavior by being treated more like a man.

The other view about how women fare at the bar of justice is that judges are more punitive toward women. They are more likely to throw the book at the female defendant, because they believe that there is a greater discrepancy between her behavior and the behavior expected of women than there is between the behavior of the male defendant and the behavior expected of men. In other words, women defendants pay for the judges' belief that it is more in man's nature to commit crimes than it is in woman's. Thus, when a judge is convinced that the woman before him has committed a crime, he is more likely to overact and punish her, not only for the specific offense, but also for transgressing against his expectations of womanly behavior.

The existence of such statutes as the indeterminate sentence for women, or the sanctioning of a procedure whereby only convicted male defendants have their minimum sentences determined by a judge at an open hearing and in the presence of counsel, while the woman's minimum sentence is decided by a parole board in a closed session in which she is not represented by counsel, are cited as evidence of the unfair, punitive treatment accorded women in the court.

In a recent article on "Discriminatory Sentencing of Women Offenders," Temen argued for passage of the Equal Rights Amendment on grounds that only such passage would make null and void all of the existing statutes that prescribe longer sentences for female offenders and that permit only females to receive an "indeterminate" sentence [Temen 1973].[a]

The views of the Superior Court of Pennsylvania in 1967 on the matter of indeterminate sentences for women is worth noting. We quote from their opinion in *Commonwealth vs. Daniel*, 210 Pa. Super. 156, 167, 232, A2d., 247, 253, (1967):

This court is of the opinion that the legislature reasonably could have concluded that indeterminant sentences should be imposed on women as a class, allowing the time of incarceration to be matched to the necessary

[a]See, e.g., State vs. Heitman, 105 Kan. 139, 181 p. 630 (1919); Ex parte Dankerton, 104 Kan. 481, 179 p. 347 (1919); Platt vs. Commonwealth, 256 Mass. 539, 152 N.E. 914 (1926); Ex parte Gosselin, 141 Me. 412, 44 A.2d 882 (1945), cert, denied sub nom. Gosselin vs. Kelley, 328 U.S. 817 (1946) Ex parte Brady, 116 Ohio St. 512, 157 N.E. 69 (1927). These cases upheld discriminatory sentencing acts against constitutional challenges.

treatment in order to provide more effective rehabilitation. Such a conclusion could be based on the physiological and psychological make-up of women, the type of crime committed by women, the relation to the criminal world, their role in society, their unique vocational skills and their reaction as a class to imprisonment, as well as the number of types of women who are sentenced to imprisonment rather than given suspended sentence.

When the Pennsylvania Supreme Court overruled the lower court's decision, it stated:

while legislative classification on the basis of sex alone did not violate the equal protection clause, it could find no reasonable justification for a statute which imposed longer sentences on women than on men convicted of the same crime (430 Pa. at 649, 243, A2d. at 403).

The Pennsylvania legislature responded by enacting a law that in essence provided for another type of indeterminate sentence for women. The law states that women alone would not have their minimum sentence determined by the court. The present procedure in Pennsylvania entitles a male offender to have his minimum sentence set by a judge at an open hearing during which representation by counsel is constitutionally mandated. But a woman's minimum sentence is decided by a parole board at a closed session, where she has no representation or any other procedural rights.

Upon reviewing the Daniel case in Pennsylvania and other cases in New Jersey, Maryland, Maine, Ohio, Iowa, and Massachusetts, Temen concluded that the courts are not the most appropriate or most efficient means for achieving equality of rights for women under the Fifth and Fourteenth Amendments; and that ratification of the Equal Rights Amendment is the most efficient way of bringing about an end to discrimination on the basis of sex.

The remainder of this chapter focuses on those data that describe rates of convictions and types of sentences received by men and women who are accused of having committed the same type of offense. Unlike the statistics that describe male and female arrest rates that are available in the *Uniform Crime Report,* there are no comprehensive judicial statistics that describe the relative conviction rates for men and women within each of the state court systems. California provides the best data on convictions and sentencing of any of the states, and in this chapter we draw heavily on the California data. Ohio also maintains some statistics by sex, and those are also considered. But a mail survey of the forty-eight other state court systems failed to turn up any other judicial statistics for which it was possible to compare conviction rates between men and women.

Since 1963 the administrative office of the United States courts has published an annual report that describes how defendants are disposed of in the eighty-nine United States district courts. These reports contain statistics that describe the proportion of men and women convicted by category of offense.

The offense categories included in these reports are:

Class I: *Fraud* (included frauds occurring against lending and credit institutions, Veteran Administration, Railroad Retirement Act, and Social Security act); *Embezzlement* (included embezzlement of bank or post funds, public money or property, lending, credit, and insurance institutions, by officers of a carrier in interstate commerce, and embezzlement by officers of labor organizations); *Obscene mail:* covers obscene mail or transmitting obscene matter in interstate commerce. Class II: *Income tax fraud:* covers evasion, failure to file, etc. income tax; *Other fraud:* frauds connected with bankruptcy, excise tax, false persovation, nationality laws, passport, Commodity Credit, Security and Exchange Commission, false claims, or statements and conspiracy not otherwise classified. Class III: liquor, Internal Revenue: covers violations of Internal Revenue Liquor laws, U.S.C. Title 26. Class IV: *Theft:* included larceny and theft from banks which are federally insured and post offices, mail theft, theft of U.S. property, and theft occurring on government reservations, etc.; *Postal fraud:* includes fraud involving the use of the mails, wire, radio, etc.; *Forgery:* includes postal forgery, and forgery of obligations and securities of the United States. Class V: *Border registration of addicts and narcotic violators, Assault and Homicide:* includes simple or aggravated assault. Homicide covers first and second degree murder and manslaughter. *Miscellaneous general offenses:* includes all offenses *not* otherwise classified, such as bribery, traffic offenses, extortion, and racketeering, gambling, and lottery, kidnapping, perjury, and laws dealing with firearms and weapons, also includes arson, abortions, bigamy, disorderly conduct, and malicious destruction of property. Class VI: *Counterfeiting; Burglary:* includes all offenses connected with the burglary or breaking and entering of a bank which is federally insured, or post offices, in interstate commerce and on government reservations; *Interstate transportation of stolen property; Marijuana:* offenses involving violations of the Marijuana Tax Act: *Selective Service Act:* violators of the Universal Military Training and Service Act of 1948; *Other national defense laws; Sex offenses:* includes rape, white slave traffic, and importing alien females for prostitution or immoral purposes. Class VII: *Auto theft:* includes transportation, etc. of stolen motor vehicles or aircraft and sale or receipt of such vehicles. Class VIII: *Narcotics:* covers all violations of the Narcotic Control Act of 1956 and the Narcotic Drugs Import and Export Act; *Robbery:* covers all federally insured lending and credit institutions, banks, and postal facilities. Also includes robberies carried out in the maritime and territorial jurisdiction of the United States and robbery of government property from an officer or employee of the United States.

The limitations of these data should be obvious, especially after reading the descriptions of the offense categories upon which the statistics are based. Most defendants in the United States, be they males or females, are tried in state courts because they have broken a state law. The offenses listed represent only a small proportion of all criminal trials in the United States. For example, in one year, in 1968, about 26,000 defendants were convicted in all of the federal district courts compared to more than 47,000 defendants who were convicted in the California state courts alone. Another factor that limits the generalizability of the federal statistics for the purposes of this volume is that some of the offenses are acts that pertain specifically to men: for example, violations of the Selective Service Act. Other offenses that are included in the federal categories are ones in which organized crime must be heavily involved; and thus far, women seem to have been effectively barred from entry into organized crime.

But one use to which these federal statistics may be put is simply to compare longitudinal trends, that is, the proportions of females who have been convicted in the federal courts from 1963 through 1971. Even in this atypical context, the expectation is that women's visibility should have increased during the latter part of the sixties. Table 5-2 describes the number and proportion of female defendants who were convicted each year for all of the offense categories combined.

In the last five years from 1967 through 1971, there has been an increase of 62 percent in the over-all number of women convicted in federal district courts, compared to an increase of only 20.3 percent for males. Unfortunately, the information available from the federal courts does not provide a separate breakdown for men and women by type and length of sentence, among those who have been convicted.

Table 5-3 compares the proportion of convictions of women in selective offense categories between 1964 and 1971. Three observations may be made about these data.

1. The offenses for which the highest proportion of women have

Table 5-2

Number of Males and Females Convicted and Percentage of Females among Convictions in Eighty-Nine US District Courts: 1963-71

Year	Males Convicted	Females Convicted	Female
1963	26,914	2086	7.0
1964	26,228	2080	7.1
1965	25,975	1957	6.8
1966	24,528	1975	7.2
1967	23,766	1805	6.7
1968	23,069	2033	7.9
1969	24,060	2109	7.9
1970	25,203	2382	8.5
1971	28,581	2931	9.1
Increase 1963-71	6.2 percent	40.5 percent	30.0 percent
Increase 1967-71	20.3 percent	62.4 percent	35.0 percent

Source: Adapted from *Federal Offenders in the U.S. District Courts.* (Washington, D.C.: Administration Office of the U.S. Courts), table 17—1963, 1964, 1965, 1966, 1967, 1968, 1969, 1970, 1971.

been convicted during the entire eight-year time span are fraud, embezzlement, and forgery. They are the same offenses for which the highest proportion of women are arrested and subsequently brought to trial in the state courts.

2. Those same offenses also show the greatest increase in the proportion of females convicted from 1964 through 1971.

3. They are the types of offenses most congruent with the hypothesis that as the women's movement gains great visibility and has more of an impact on its potential constituency, female crime rates will increase, and they will increase especially in these offense categories.

The remainder of the chapter compares the proportion of men and women who were convicted and sentenced in the state of California over the past decade or so and over a shorter period of time in Ohio. As indicated earlier, California provided the major portion of the judicial statistics we have for examining how women fare in the state courts. We do not feel that it is unsound to generalize conviction rates from California to the rest of the country, because

California arrest rates approximate those for the country as a whole [Ward 1968].

Table 5-4 describes the proportion of females who have been convicted by offense categories in California superior courts from 1960 through 1972. Note that for all of the crimes combined in table 5-4, there has been a 31 percent increase in the proportion of women convicted between 1960 and 1972. There has been an increase of 29 percent in the proportion of women convicted of the violent offenses included in the Index of Serious Crimes (homicide, robbery, and assault) but a decline of 13 percent in the proportion of women convicted of the property offenses included in the index (burglary, larceny, and auto theft). Thus, even though the proportion of women arrested has increased for the property offenses contained in the index, and declined for the violent offenses, women arrested in the past few years for violent offenses are more likely to be convicted than those in the earlier part of the 1960s. But the increase in female arrest rates for Type I property offenses has not been followed by an increase in female conviction rates for those offenses.

In the Type II offenses, the level of women convictions has increased sharply for one crime: drug law violations. Indeed, we see that drug law violations in 1972 accounted for almost half (43.5 percent) of all female convictions (table 5-5).

We can compare the California judicial statistics against those obtained from Ohio for a three-year period, 1969, 1970, and 1971. Among the eight offense categories for which there are comparable data, the rank order from highest to lowest conviction rates is similar for both states in each year. Forgery has the highest proportion of female conviction rates, followed by homicide, narcotics, and theft, although not always in that order (table 5-6).

In both states, when one examines the types of offenses for which females have the highest rates of conviction among all women convicted in a given year, drug violations and forgery occupy the highest positions (table 5-7).

Table 5-8 compares the proportions of men and women who pleaded guilty, and who were found guilty, by type of offense between 1969 and 1972 in California. Note that for all offenses combined there is no greater likelihood that men will plead guilty than women; indeed, the proportion of men convicted is not significantly higher than the proportion of women. For example, for every eleven

Table 5-3

Percentage of Females among Convictions by Specific Offense Categories: Eighty-nine US District Courts: 1964-71[a]

Offense category	1964 Number	1964 Percent Females	1965 Number	1965 Percent Females	1966 Number	1966 Percent Females	1967 Number	1967 Percent Females	1968 Number	1968 Percent Females
Class I:										
Fraud	666	12.4	515	16.7	555	18.9	300	18.7	250	26.4
Embezzlement	1,231	20.7	1,207	19.7	1,148	21.0	1,220	24.5	1,231	24.6
Class II:										
Income tax fraud	597	6.7	574	7.3	593	5.2	542	5.7	498	6.8
Other fraud	581	7.1	489	4.7	404	4.7	357	7.3	287	4.9
Class IV:										
Theft	2,418	10.5	2,256	10.8	2,223	9.7	2,137	8.9	2,282	10.6
Postal fraud	413	12.1	418	14.4	385	11.2	341	14.7	359	15.0
Forgery	2,517	22.4	2,117	21.9	1,958	23.5	1,642	24.1	1,787	24.5
Class V:										
Assault, Homicide	233	8.6	214	8.4	254	2.8	249	3.6	268	6.3
Class VIII:										
Narcotics	919	10.6	1,116	10.0	1,052	11.7	914	12.9	953	9.4
Robbery	524	3.4	660	2.0	577	5.5	703	2.6	862	3.8

Offense category	1969		1970		1971		Average rate change	
	Number	Percent Females	Number	Percent Females	Number	Percent Females	1964-71	1967-71
Class I:								
Fraud	257	21.8	236	33.1	235	28.1	+2.24	+2.35
Embezzlement	1,421	26.4	1,602	27.3	1,940	26.7	+ .86	+ .55
Class II:								
Income tax fraud	502	5.2	483	7.7	693	7.9	+ .17	+ .55
Other fraud	271	8.5	282	8.2	455	7.3	+ .03	0
Class IV:								
Theft	2,281	9.8	2,488	10.5	3,088	11.8	+ .19	+ .73
Postal fraud	405	9.9	387	13.7	496	14.9	+ .40	+ .05
Forgery	1,441	25.3	1,741	26.3	2,042	27.1	+ .67	+ .75
Class V:								
Assault, Homicide	354	7.1	390	7.4	364	6.0	− .37	+ .60
Class VIII:								
Narcotics	1,007	11.9	919	10.9	1,158	11.3	+ .10	− .40
Robbery	961	4.0	1,002	3.4	1,359	5.3	+ .27	+ .68

[a]Total number of persons, male and female, convicted.
Source: Adapted from *Federal Offenders in the U.S. District Courts* (Washington, D.C.: Administration Office of the U.S. Courts), tables 17, 1963, 1964, 1965, 1966, 1967, 1968, 1969, 1970, 1971.

Table 5-4
California: Percentage of Females among Convictions in Superior Courts, 1960-64 and 1966-72[a]

Offense	1960-64		1966		1967		1968	
	Number	Percent Females	Number	Percent Females	Number	Percent Females	Number	Percent Females
Homicide and manslaughter	2,557	12.4	656	12.7	764	14.5	851	14.7
Robbery	8,756	2.6	1,666	3.2	2,721	5.0	3,050	4.7
Assault	7,860	8.2	2,553	8.6	2,650	10.4	3,284	11.0
Burglary	24,650	2.4	5,704	3.2	7,691	4.1	8,326	4.4
Larceny-theft	16,450	12.2	3,685	16.4	3,563	14.8	3,675	16.7
Auto theft	9,596	1.8	2,569	2.2	2,639	2.2	2,950	3.1
Forgery and checks	23,375	16.6	4,810	20.4	4,432	22.5	4,818	24.8
Drug law violations	14,439	10.3	5,334	9.6	9,877	11.3	12,889	12.0
Violent crimes	19,173	6.2	4,875	7.3	6,135	8.5	7,185	8.8
Property crimes	50,696	5.5	11,958	7.1	13,893	6.5	15,451	6.9
All crimes	136,083	8.3	36,844	8.9	41,027	9.7	47,277	10.5

Offense	1969 Number	1969 Percent Females	1970 Number	1970 Percent Females	1971 Number	1971 Percent Females	1972 Number	1972 Percent Females
Homicide and manslaughter	731	12.3	850	12.2	940	13.2	1,047	13.8
Robbery	2,106	3.9	2,207	3.1	2,719	3.6	2,753	3.7
Assault	3,495	10.1	3,373	9.2	3,654	10.3	3,681	9.6
Burglary	6,362	3.6	6,499	3.4	7,913	3.4	7,315	3.7
Larceny-theft	2,102	13.2	2,410	11.7	2,676	11.1	2,645	9.9
Auto theft	3,018	2.8	2,485	2.9	2,529	3.2	2,132	2.4
Forgery and checks	4,476	27.0	4,118	26.9	4,107	28.4	3,493	27.7
Drug law violations	18,367	12.3	18,672	13.9	20,808	14.4	15,954	14.5
Violent crimes	6,332	8.3	6,430	7.5	7,313	8.2	7,481	8.0
Property crimes	11,482	5.2	11,394	5.1	13,118	4.9	12,092	4.8
All crimes	50,123	10.9	49,679	11.1	55,734	11.2	48,730	10.9

[a]Total number of persons, male and female, convicted.
Note: Data for 1965 missing.

Source: Adapted from Bureau of Criminal Statistics, *Crime and Delinquency in California* (Sacramento, Calif.: Dept. of Justice, State of California, 1960-64, 1966-72).

Table 5-5
California: Distribution of Convictions among Specific Offenses, Females Convicted in Superior Courts: 1960-64, 1966-72[a]

Offense Category	1960-64	1966	1967	1968	1969	1970	1971	1972
Homicide and Manslaughter	2.8	2.6	2.8	2.5	1.7	1.9	2.0	2.7
Robbery	2.0	1.8	3.5	2.9	1.5	1.3	1.6	1.9
Assault	5.7	7.1	7.0	7.2	6.5	5.6	6.0	6.6
Burglary	5.2	6.2	8.0	7.4	4.2	4.1	4.3	5.1
Larceny-Theft	17.7	18.3	13.3	12.3	5.1	5.1	4.7	5.0
Auto Theft	1.5	2.0	1.5	1.8	1.5	1.3	1.3	1.0
Forgery and Checks	34.3	28.7	25.1	24.0	22.2	20.0	18.6	18.2
Drug Law Violations	13.2	16.4	28.1	30.9	41.6	35.3	47.8	43.5
Violent Crimes[b]	10.5	11.5	13.3	12.6	9.7	8.8	9.6	11.2
Property Crimes[c]	24.4	26.5	22.8	21.5	10.8	10.5	10.3	11.1
All Crimes	100	100	100	100	100	100	100	100

[a]Numbers in columns do not add up to 100 because some crimes are left out.
[b]Homicide, Robbery, and Assault.
[c]Burglary, Larceny, and Auto Theft.

Source: Adapted from Bureau of Criminal Statistics, *Crime and Delinquency in California* (Sacramento, Calif.: Dept. of Justice, State of California, 1960-1972).

Table 5-6
Percentage of Females Convicted in California and Ohio: 1969-71

	1969		1970		1971	
Offense	California	Ohio	California	Ohio	California	Ohio
Homicide and Manslaughter	12.3	14.9	12.2	10.5	13.2	12.7
Robbery	3.9	4.6	3.1	4.2	3.6	4.1
Assault	10.1	7.1	9.2	5.9	10.3	7.4
Burglary	3.6	1.9	3.4	2.0	3.4	1.7
Larceny-Theft	13.2	9.3	11.7	10.6	11.1	8.8
Forgery and Checks	27.0	19.4	26.9	19.1	28.4	21.2
Narcotic Laws Violations	12.3	12.8	13.9	12.6	14.4	12.8
All Crimes	10.9	8.2	11.1	8.1	11.2	8.4

Source: Adapted from Dept. of Mental Health and Mental Retardation, *Ohio Judicial Criminal Statistics*. (Columbus, O.: Bureau of Statistics), 1969 (table 4, p. 14); 1970 (table 3, p. 12); 1971 (table 3, p. 20). Bureau of Criminal Statistics, *Crime and Delinquency in California* (Sacramento, Calif.: Dept. of Justice, State of California, 1969-71).

Table 5-7
Distribution of Convictions in Percentages among Specific Crime Categories for Females: California and Ohio: 1969-71

	1969		1970		1971	
Offense[a]	California	Ohio	California	Ohio	California	Ohio
Homicide and Manslaughter	1.7	4.3	1.9	2.7	2.0	2.8
Robbery	1.5	5.8	1.3	4.6	1.6	4.6
Assault	6.5	5.0	5.6	3.7	6.0	4.4
Burglary	4.2	6.4	4.1	6.9	4.3	5.4
Larceny-Theft	5.1	11.7	5.1	14.4	4.7	11.0
Forgery and Checks	22.2	23.1	20.0	22.7	18.6	26.3
Narcotic Laws Violations	41.6	12.7	35.3	17.9	47.8	22.3
All Crimes	100	100	100	100	100	100

[a]Numbers in columns do not add up to 100 because some crimes have been omitted.

Source: Adapted from Dept. of Mental Health and Mental Retardation, *Ohio Judicial Criminal Statistics* (Columbus, O.: Bureau of Statistics), 1969 (table 4, p. 14); 1970 (table 3, p. 12); 1971 (table 3, p. 20). Bureau of Criminal Statistics, *Crime and Delinquency in California* (Sacramento, Calif.: State of California, 1969-1971).

Table 5-8
California: Percentage of Persons Charged Who Plead Guilty, and Who are Convicted[a] 1969-72

Offense Charged		1969			1970		
		No. of Persons Charged	Percent of Guilty Pleas	Percent of Convic-tions	No. of Persons Charged	Percent of Guilty Pleas	Percent of Convic-tions
Murder	Female	123	17.7	60.2	113	44.4	75.2
	Male	609	47.1	83.6	710	46.5	85.4
Manslaughter	Female	18	50.0	72.2	15	66.7	80.0
	Male	67	61.2	80.6	68	63.2	80.9
Robbery	Female	211	53.6	79.6	191	48.7	79.6
	Male	3094	59.4	87.1	3494	58.5	87.3
Assault	Female	430	50.9	82.3	372	50.5	79.3
	Male	3163	54.6	86.2	3026	56.7	83.7
Burglary	Female	440	64.5	84.5	478	58.8	87.2
	Male	8651	68.8	91.3	8938	67.0	90.3
Theft	Female	346	65.6	80.1	354	49.4	68.9
	Male	1778	65.0	84.2	2284	60.6	82.5
Embezzlement	Female	5	100.0	100.0	2	50.0	100.0
	Male	15	73.3	86.7	14	85.7	100.0
Petty Theft	Female	39	82.0	97.4	39	69.2	94.9
	Male	226	67.7	94.2	215	73.5	95.3
Fraud	Female	16	43.8	75.0	24	41.7	62.5
	Male	23	73.9	95.7	41	73.2	80.5
Auto Theft	Female	115	49.6	72.2	81	51.9	72.8
	Male	3129	64.3	86.7	2500	62.4	86.0
Forgery and Checks	Female	1335	80.0	94.0	1236	78.0	92.4
	Male	3590	80.8	93.4	3303	77.6	93.0
Drug Law Violations	Female	3016	56.7	76.4	3389	55.1	77.8
	Male	19519	60.7	66.0	19776	57.9	82.3
Drunken Driving	Female	57	72.0	89.5	48	79.2	95.8
	Male	581	75.9	94.3	663	74.7	95.8
All Crimes	Female	6689	62.5	81.4	6850	58.9	80.8
	Male	51713	63.9	86.4	51721	61.7	85.3
Violent Crimes[b]	Female	782	46.3	77.9	691	49.3	78.7
	Male	6933	56.2	86.4	7298	56.7	85.6
Property Crimes[c]	Female	2296	73.2	88.9	2214	67.8	86.5
	Male	17412	70.1	90.2	17295	67.6	89.2

[a]Convictions include Guilty Pleas.
[b]Murder, Manslaughter, Robbery and Assault.
[c]Burglary, Theft, Embezzlement, Petty Theft, Fraud, Auto Theft, Forgery and Checks.
[d]Average Male-to-Female Ratio of Guilty Plea Proportions.

	1971			1972			
No. of Persons Charged	Percent of Guilty Pleas	Percent of Convic- tions	No. of Persons Charged	Percent of Guilty Pleas	Percent of Convic- tions	3[d]	4[e]
143	46.9	78.3	170	48.2	77.6		
796	44.2	84.2	906	42.5	86.3	1.4	1.2
12	83.3	83.3	19	47.4	68.4		
65	75.4	83.1	69	56.5	73.9	1.1	1.1
234	60.7	79.9	193	66.1	80.0		
4302	64.4	87.5	4184	67.1	88.9	1.1	1.1
427	55.0	82.2	415	61.4	82.4		
3253	58.4	83.5	3603	64.7	85.2	1.1	1.0
541	70.8	82.4	513	72.7	85.0		
10515	75.3	91.8	9478	79.4	91.7	1.1	1.1
301	69.1	79.1	257	68.1	82.5		
2389	67.9	83.8	2007	72.5	86.2	1.1	1.1
3	100.0	100.0	5	60.0	100.0		
15	86.7	100.0	11	72.7	81.8	1.1	0.9
42	81.0	95.2	46	87.0	97.8		
269	79.9	93.7	272	82.7	95.2	1.0	1.0
9	66.7	88.9	61	77.0	86.9		
48	68.8	83.3	91	70.3	84.6	1.3	1.1
87	69.0	82.8	63	58.7	68.3		
2507	72.0	88.1	1947	76.6	89.3	1.2	1.2
1285	84.7	93.0	1058	87.2	94.6		
3223	83.6	93.3	2808	86.4	93.1	1.0	1.0
3850	61.4	79.2	2931	64.5	79.9		
21406	66.2	84.3	16136	70.3	85.3	1.1	1.0
58	82.8	94.8	71	81.7	100.0		
735	77.0	94.7	645	76.9	92.7	1.0	1.0
7616	66.2	82.2	6394	69.2	83.2		
56966	68.8	86.8	49567	72.1	87.6	1.0	1.1
816	55.6	80.9	797	59.3	80.7		
8416	60.2	85.6	8762	63.5	87.0	1.1	1.1
2268	78.6	88.3	2003	79.8	89.6		
18966	75.4	90.6	16614	79.4	91.0	1.0	1.0

[e]Average Male-to-Female Ratio of Conviction Proportions.

Source: Bureau of Criminal Statistics, *Crime and Delinquency in California* (Sacramento, Calif.: Dept. of Justice, State of California, 1969-1972).

Table 5-9
Comparison of Average Ratios of Male to Female Conviction Rates, California and Ohio: 1969-71[a]

Offense Charged	Male-to-Female Ratio of Percent Convicted (Includes Guilty Pleas)		Male-to-Female Ratio of Percent Convicted Who Plead Not Guilty
	Ohio	California	California
Murder and Manslaughter	1.35	1.18	1.25
Robbery	1.08	1.10	1.32
Assault	1.23	1.04	1.06
Burglary	1.29	1.08	1.32
Larceny and Theft	1.13	1.10	1.35
Petty Theft		0.99	0.93
Auto Theft		1.15	1.62
Embezzlement and Fraud	0.94	1.04	0.96
Forgery	0.98	1.00	1.27
Drug Law Violations	1.12	1.00	1.19
Drunken Driving		1.00	1.01
All Crimes	1.08	1.11	1.21
Violent Crimes[b]	1.22	1.11	1.16
Property Crimes[c]	1.08	1.13	1.29

[a]There are some differences in Crime Classifications:
    Ohio specifies Aggravated Assault, whereas California specifies Assault.
    Ohio specifies Forgery and Counterfeiting; California uses the category Forgery and Checks.

[b]Murder, Manslaughter, Robbery and Assault.

[c]Burglary, Theft, Embezzlement and Fraud, Petty Theft, Auto Theft, Forgery. (In Ohio, Petty Theft is not included.)

Source: Adapted from Dept. of Mental Health and Mental Retardation, *Ohio Judicial Criminal Statistics* (Columbus, O.: Bureau of Statistics), 1969 (table 4, p. 14); 1970 (table 3, p. 12); 1971 (table 3, p. 20). Bureau of Criminal Statistics, *Crime and Delinquency in California* (Sacramento, Calif.: Dept. of Justice, State of California, 1969-71).

men convicted of violent offenses, so are ten women; and for property offenses the ratios are equal.

We were also able to compare the male-to-female ratio of convictions in Ohio and California over approximately the same time periods for most of the same offense categories. (The California data include 1972; Ohio data end with 1971.) For comparable offenses, California appears to be more even-handed than Ohio. The biggest differences occur in the categories of homicide and manslaughter, burglary, and drug law violations. But note also that women in California who plead *not guilty* are more likely to be acquitted than

are men. Women accused of such typically male offenses as robbery, burglary, and auto theft are treated at least as preferentially as
women accused of larceny, an offense more typical of women.
These data, then, fail to support the Nagel-Weitzman theory that
women who commit more "manly type offenses" pay the price for
their behavior by being treated more like men.

Unfortunately, judicial statistics such as those shown in tables
5-8 and 5-9 are not available for earlier years, so we can not say that
the disparity in preferential treatment for women is on the wane, or
that it has remained unchanged. These data allow us to say only that
women as recently as 1972 seem to be receiving some preferential
treatment at the bar of justice, and on the basis of the available data
to conclude that the eyes of justice are neither blinded nor fully
opened; rather, they seem to be open just enough to be able to
discern the sex of the defendant and to allow that characteristic to
influence the decisions to some extent.

6

The Forgotten Offender[a]

The woman in prison has been referred to as "the forgotten offender" by those who want to call attention to her plight and to bring about changes in her situation. Part of the reason for the lack of interest in female inmates is that there are so few of them. In 1971, about eighteen out of 100 persons arrested for a serious crime was a woman. In the same year about nine out of 100 persons convicted for a serious crime was a woman, but only about three out of every 100 persons sentenced to a federal or state prison was a woman. As of December 1970, of the approximately 196,000 inmates in state and federal prisons, 5600 were women. At the present time there are three federal institutions for women and twenty-three for men. There are forty state institutions for women and 250 for men.

Another reason for the lack of interest is because the women inmates themselves have called so little attention to their situation. Prison reforms, and indeed public and official interest in prisoners, are strongly influenced by the amount of disruption and violence that occur inside the prisons. Prisoners need to riot, to destroy property, to endanger the lives of guards and fellow inmates, to submit a list of demands for reforming the institution, before they are likely to receive much attention. Following such activities, the public demands an investigation, the governor appoints a "blue ribbon fact-finding commission," and prison officials acknowledge that reforms are needed and will be made. Along with many other forms

---

[a]Unlike other issues with which this book is concerned, female inmates in prisons have received quite a lot of study. Since well back into the nineteenth century, social reformers, clinicians, and law enforcement officers have been concerned about the physical conditions and facilities under which women inmates must live, the types of educational and vocational training programs available to them, the quality and background of the personnel who supervise them, and the social organization within the prison. The latter topic has attracted particular attention in the last two or three decades with the publication of such works as Rose Giallombardo's *Society of Women* (1966), Ward and Kassebaum's *Women's Prisons* (1965), and most recently, Kathryn Burkhart's *Women in Prison* (1973). These books, especially the first two, place great emphasis on the informal organization that develops among the inmates and the types of obligations and responsibilities, especially sexual, that prisoners develop with one another. But much of this literature on female inmates, while interesting in itself, is not directly relevant to the major issues that this book addresses.

of social unrest, the sixties and the early seventies witnessed a number of serious prison riots in many large federal and state institutions in which inmates and guards were killed. But throughout this period the number of women's institutions that engaged in such behavior was practically nil, and the amount of publicity and interest that such institutions received was proportionate to their failure to call attention to themselves.

Still a third reason for the lack of interest in women prisoners is that the crimes women commit usually inconvenience society less than male crimes. The overwhelming majority of women offenders have not been involved with organized crime, with crime involving high losses of property, or with crimes that have endangered large numbers of people.

One of the anticipated by-products of the contemporary women's movement is that it will make the woman more equal before the bar of justice; in effect, more women will be sentenced to prison than have been in the past. Carolyn Handy, of the United States Commission on Civil Rights, claims that there is a visible trend toward equal penalties for equal crimes with more and longer prison terms for women resulting.

In table 6-1 we see the proportion of women compared to men who were sentenced to all of the federal and state institutions for selective years from 1950 to 1970. Note that what increase there has been in the proportion of women sentenced to prison has come solely from the three federal institutions, where only a small minority of all the women are sent. But the trend for the state institutions is in the opposite direction. There has been a decline in the proportion of women sentenced to state institutions over the past two decades.

These results do not support the "more equal treatment" hypothesis. There is no consistent trend that indicates that the courts have been committing a higher proportion of women to prisons in the past few years than they have one or two decades ago. Female commitments to state institutions dropped in 1967 and rose in 1968 and 1969, but then dropped again in 1970 by about the same percent that they dropped between 1965 and 1967. There may have been an increase in the proportion of women committed to federal institutions from 1965 through 1970, but the numbers are too small to assume that they reflect a change in policy.

Commitment data by sex over some periods of time are available for New York and California, the two most populous states. The

Table 6-1
Population of Sentenced Prisoners by Type of Institution and Sex with Relative Percentages of Male and Female Prisoners: 1950-70

Year	Male	Female	Federal Institutions		State Institutions	
			Percent Male	Percent Female	Percent Male	Percent Female
1950	66,161 (95.2%)	3,312 (4.8%)	96.7	3.3	94.9	5.1
1955	74,368 (94.8%)	4,046 (5.2%)	96.3	3.7	94.5	5.5
1960	84,264 (95.1%)	4,311 (4.9%)	95.9	4.1	95.0	5.0
1965	83,241 (95.1%)	4,264 (4.9%)	95.8	4.2	95.0	5.0
1967	74,400 (95.6%)	3,450 (4.4%)	95.8	4.2	95.5	4.5
1968	68,426 (95.0%)	3,632 (5.0%)	95.5	4.5	94.9	5.1
1969	71,479 (95.0%)	3,798 (5.0%)	95.6	4.4	94.8	5.2
1970	75,692 (95.4%)	3,659 (4.6%)	95.4	4.6	95.3	4.7
Percent Change in Proportions, 1950-70	0	+.05	−0.01	+39.40	+0.40	−7.80

Source: Adapted from *National Prisoner Statistics Bulletin* (Washington, D.C.: U.S. Dept. of Justice, Bureau of Prisons, April 1972), table 5, p. 8.

New York data (table 6-2), which are based on the number and proportions of women committed to New York State correctional institutions for each year from 1963 to 1971, show that the over-all proportion of females committed has *declined* during this period. The highest proportion of female commitments in a given year occurred in 1966; after that the proportion declined to its current level of 3.4. The numbers for each year for specific offenses are so small (for example, in 1971, three women were committed for murder, seven for burglary, and eighteen for grand larceny) as to make it foolhardy to project trends on the basis of them. But when one examines the proportion of women committed for all felony offenses in a given year, it is clear that there has been no dramatic increase since the women's movement or the equal rights movement has surfaced.

Table 6-2

Percentage of Females among New Commitments to New York State Correctional Institutions, by Type of Offense: 1963-71[a]

Reason for commitment	1963		1964		1965		1966		1967	
	Number	Percent Female	Number	Percent Female	Number	Percent Female	Number	Percent Female	Number	Percent Female
Murder	74	2.7	69	0	64	3.1	70	1.4	40	2.5
Homicide, negligent, non-negligent	262	13.4	300	10.7	280	12.1	334	12.0	320	9.4
Robbery	760	1.3	757	.7	820	1.7	647	.9	751	.9
Burglary	538	1.1	465	.9	455	.4	353	1.7	360	.3
Felonious assault	476	4.4	400	3.3	415	5.5	392	5.3	377	2.7
Grand larceny	572	5.2	582	4.8	681	3.4	492	4.5	491	4.3
Auto theft	169	0	167	0	135	0	105	.9	106	0
Dangerous drugs	514	13.0	427	7.7	379	9.5	474	10.5	589	5.0
Forgery	123	9.8	91	9.9	92	7.6	58	17.2	77	10.4
All felonies	3,839	5.1	3,558	3.7	3,585	4.3	3,193	5.3	3,357	3.4

Reason for commitment	1968		1969		1970		1971	
	Number	Percent Female	Number	Percent Female	Number	Percent Female	Number	Percent Female
Murder	48	0	45	4.4	68	2.9	101	3.0
Homicide, negligent, non-negligent	378	10.0	472	7.8	515	7.0	602	6.0
Robbery	944	1.0	1,277	1.4	1,190	1.0	1,553	1.4
Burglary	413	1.5	445	.9	414	.2	431	1.6
Felonious assault	311	5.1	274	3.3	246	3.3	272	2.6
Grand larceny	290	2.0	229	5.2	183	6.0	199	9.0
Auto theft	53	3.8	28	0	28	0	22	0
Dangerous drugs	385	3.1	431	3.5	470	6.4	690	5.5
Forgery	55	20.0	71	11.3	56	5.4	73	9.6
All felonies	3,118	3.3	3,610	3.1	3,522	3.1	4,353	3.4

[a]Total number of persons, male and female, convicted.

Source: Adapted from *Characteristics of New Commitments* (State of New York, Department of Corrections, 1963-71).

The California data, which describe the proportion of men and women prisoners in all of the California correctional institutions from 1945 through 1972 (table 6-3), do not show a marked increase in the proportion of women prisoners from the late sixties to 1972. Indeed, there were about the same proportion of women inmates in 1972 as there were in the 1950s.

For 1967-69, we can compare the proportion of men and women committed to California correctional institutions based on the number convicted for specific offenses (table 6-4). Note first that among the men and women convicted for all serious offenses, more than twice as many men are committed to prison as are women. Women are more likely to receive "equal treatment" for violent offenses than they are for property offenses. Theft and narcotics are offenses for which women seem to receive the most preferential treatment. Unfortunately, statistics such as these are not available over longer periods of time, so we cannot see whether the "preferential" status that women enjoyed in the late sixties remained relatively stable or whether these ratios in fact represent a decline in their preferential status. But the years shown in table 6-4 are worth careful attention, because they are part of that era that should have reflected the shift toward "more equal" treatment that the women's movement was supposed to influence. There is no indication in those data, as there are none in the data based on percentages of women in correctional institutions, that women are being treated "more equally" by the courts, when commitment to prison is at issue.

The Equal Rights Amendment and Women in Prison

One of the targets of the equal rights movement is the American prison system, which provides separate facilities for men and women. Separate prisons were established for women beginning in the 1880s as a reform intended to give them the benefit of rehabilitation then being sought for young men and boys in new reformatories [Singer 1973, p. 295].

With the exception of Pennsylvania, Florida, Mississippi, and New Mexico, every state has segregated their male and female prisoners by housing them in separate facilities. The four states

Table 6-3
Prisoners by Sex and Year in California: 1945-72

Year	Total	Men	Women	Percent Women
1945	6,628	6,436	192	2.9
1946	7,839	7,592	247	3.2
1947	9,044	8,759	282	3.1
1948	10,084	9,776	308	2.5
1949	10,899	10,581	318	2.9
1950	11,598	11,273	325	2.8
1951	11,939	11,551	388	3.2
1952	13,169	12,754	415	3.2
1953	14,149	13,699	450	3.2
1954	15,376	14,832	544	3.5
1955	15,230	14,673	557	3.7
1956	15,532	14,922	610	3.9
1957	16,918	16,249	669	4.0
1958	19,202	18,472	730	3.8
1959	19,299	18,490	809	4.2
1960	21,660	20,831	829	3.8
1961	23,927	23,058	869	3.6
1962	24,032	23,136	896	3.7
1963	26,133	25,272	861	3.3
1964	26,483	25,513	970	3.7
1965	26,325	25,143	1,182	4.5
1966	27,467	26,248	1,219	4.4
1967	27,741	26,658	1,083	3.9
1968	28,462	27,396	1,066	3.7
1969	27,535	26,494	1,041	3.8
1970	25,033	24,105	928	3.7
1971	20,294	19,403	891	4.4
1972	19,773	18,994	779	3.9

Source: Adapted from Bureau of Criminal Statistics, *Crime and Delinquency in California* (Sacramento, Calif.: Dept. of Justice, State of California, 1945-1972).

maintain men and women in separate wings of the same institutions and segregate them within daily activities. Advocates of the Equal Rights Amendment who have directed their interests at the female offender have claimed that the same reasoning that was persuasive to the Supreme Court in *Brown* vs. *the Board of Education* (that segregation by itself denies to blacks equal opportunities and equality in their educational experiences) applies to women because of the maintenance of a separate prison system. Schools that segregate by race and prisons that segregate by sex are basically discriminatory.

The authors of a note in the Yale Law Journal (May 1973) claimed that although the Supreme Court had as yet not made the same determination concerning segregation on the basis of sex that it

Table 6-4
California: Percentage of Convicted Persons Sentenced to Prison, by Crime and Sex: 1967-69

Offense Category		1967 No. of Persons Convicted	1967 Percent Committed to Prison	1968 No. of Persons Convicted	1968 Percent Committed to Prison	1969 No. of Persons Convicted	1969 Percent Committed to Prison	Average Ratio of Male to Female Imprisonment Rate
Homicide	Female	111	27.0	125	36.8	90	34.4	1.5
	Male	653	44.9	726	45.0	641	59.1	
Robbery	Female	137	16.1	144	16.7	82	28.0	1.9
	Male	2,584	36.0	2,906	31.2	2,024	42.1	
Assault	Female	276	7.6	361	5.3	352	6.0	1.9
	Male	2,374	13.4	2,923	11.5	3,143	11.3	
Burglary	Female	319	7.5	370	3.5	231	7.4	1.6
	Male	7,372	11.4	8,156	9.5	6,131	11.8	
Theft	Female	526	8.0	612	7.8	277	16.6	3.6
	Male	3,037	21.1	1,196	50.6	1,825	28.8	
Forgery and Checks	Female	996	8.3	1,196	5.7	1,209	3.6	2.3
	Male	3,436	15.7	3,622	12.8	3,267	10.0	
Narcotics	Female	1,115	0.9	1,542	3.3	2,263	2.1	4.1
	Male	8,762	7.6	11,347	5.6	16,104	4.6	
All Above Crimes	Female	3,480	7.4	4,350	6.2	4,504	5.1	2.2
	Male	28,218	15.0	30,876	13.1	33,135	11.8	
Violent Crimes[a]	Female	524	13.9	630	14.1	524	14.3	1.9
	Male	5,611	27.4	6,555	23.9	5,808	27.3	
Property Crimes[b]	Female	1,841	8.1	2,178	5.9	1,717	6.2	2.2
	Male	13,845	14.6	12,974	14.1	11,223	14.0	

[a]Homicide, Robbery, and Assault.
[b]Burglary, Theft, and Forgery and Checks.

Source: Adapted from Bureau of Criminal Statistics. *Crime and Delinquency in California* (Sacramento, Calif.: Dept. of Justice, State of California, 1967, 1968, 1969).

made for segregation on the basis of color (separate, by its nature cannot be equal) the ERA would compel such a result.

The authors also recognize that because of the much greater numbers of male inmates, application of a "sexually-neutral classification scheme" could cause certain problems.

For example, in a particular state system a female inmate might find herself one of only two or three women in an integrated "population" with hundreds of men. Such gross numerical disparity may run afoul of the Eighth Amendment's prohibition against cruel and unusual punishment, the inmate's right of privacy, and her right to equal protection of the laws. Balancing these rights in urgent situations, the courts might allow a woman to choose not to be confined in a particular institution. Incarcerating at least five or ten women in each institution should, however, provide sufficient same-sex companionship without significantly hindering the process of integration [Arditi et al. 1973, p. 1265].[b]

That women prisoners comprise such a tiny proportion of all prisoners has affected the lives of women incarcerated in many important ways. Indeed, the effect begins from the moment the woman is sentenced. Because there are fewer female institutions, when a woman is committed, she is likely to be sent much farther from her community than is her male counterpart. No state operates more than one female penal institution, and eight states do not have any prisons for women. She thus experiences greater difficulty in keeping track of her possessions and her family. None of the women's prisons have any provisions for women with children, although the majority of women in prison at any given time are mothers. The Women's Bureau of the US Department of Labor estimates that 70 percent of the inmates in the federal system are women.

The superintendent at the California Institution for Women stated:

Almost all the women who come to prison have husbands and children. If a man goes to prison, the wife stays home and he usually has his family to return to and the household is there when he gets out. But women generally don't have family support from the outside. Very few men are going to sit around and take care of the children and be there when she gets back. So—to send a woman to prison means you are virtually going to disrupt her family. She knows that when she gets out she probably won't have a husband waiting for her. It will really mean starting her life over again.

[b]Reprinted by permission of the Yale Law Journal Company and Fred B. Rothman & Company from *The Yale Law Journal*, Vol. 82, pp. 1229-1273.

It is also more difficult for her to communicate with her lawyer and to gain access to her parole board.

The size of the female prison population also affects the heterogeneity of the populations within women's prisons. Women's prisons contain a more heterogeneous population than do prisons for men. They include a wider range of ages than do the male prisons, and there is less differentiation by types of offenders. All but nine states have more than one institution for male offenders, and the decision about which type of institution to commit is based on age and type of offense.

But not all of the differences between men's and women's institutions that derive from the principle of sexual segregation result in women experiencing more negative treatment. The stereotypes that are held of women in the larger society provide some advantages to the female inmates. As Burkhart (1973, p. 367) points out:

Women just weren't considered as dangerous or as violent as men. So —rather than the mass penitentiary housing used for men—women's prisons were designed as a domestic model—with each woman having a "room" of her own. Often no more than stretches of open fields or wire fences separate women prisoners and the "free world"—armed guards are rarely visible. Just like women outside, a woman prisoner would be confined to "the home."

"The home" planned for women was a cottage that was built to house 20 to 30 women—who would cook their own food in a "cottage kitchen." The cottages in most states were built to contain a living room, dining room and 1 or 2 small reading rooms.[c]

Physically, then, female institutions are usually more attractive and more pleasant than the security oriented institutions for men. They tend to be located in more pastoral settings, and they tend not to have the gun towers, the concrete walls, and the barbed wire that so often characterize the male institutions. Women inmates usually have more privacy than men; they tend to have single rooms; they may wear street clothes rather than prison uniforms; they may decorate their rooms with bedspreads and curtains provided by the prison. Toilet and shower facilities also reflect a greater concern for women's privacy. Because women prisoners are perceived as less dangerous and less escape prone than men, most states also allow them more trips outside the prison than they do their male counterparts.

Burkhart (1973, p. 153) quotes the following passage from *The Clarion,* a convict newspaper published at the California Institution for Women at Frontera:

We are not physically abused, we are demoralized drop by drop, that's all. We are not physically uncomfortable, we are involved in a psychological war about 10 out of every 24 hrs, that's all. We are not starving to death from self-inflicted and other kinds of pain we live with; we are not cold from lack of proper clothing or heating. We are freezing from the cold, icy reality that even though we've done time for a crime, we will pay for it for the rest of our lives.

Advocates of the ERA recognize the preferential treatment accorded to women inmates and oppose it.

In terms of physical facilities and the general prison environment most women now receive better treatment than their male counterparts. The ERA would eliminate this differential by subjecting both men and women to the same physical surrounding in sexually integrated institutions. Ideally, the equalization would be up to the level presently enjoyed by the women. But, in most states, this would require either renovation of all or most all existing male institutions or the construction of all new facilities designed to meet the high standards now found in most female prisons. Again, if the state faces an economic roadblock to equalizing up, the ERA would tolerate equalization down to a lower, more economically feasible level [Arditi, et al., May 1973, p. 1266].

One of the major sources of criticism of women's prisons today is the quality and variety of the educational and vocational training programs available in those institutions. Based on a survey they conducted among inmates in two of the three federal prisons for women, the Women's Bureau of the Department of Labor concluded that 85 percent of the inmates want more job training; and 80 percent want more educational opportunities than are available at those institutions [Koontz 1971, p. 7]. Nine out of ten of the respondents also said that they expected to work to support themselves, when they were released. A majority also expected that they would support others who were dependent upon them.

Yet examination of the vocational training opportunities available at most women's prisons suggests that those responsible for the programs hold a view of the roles women ought to play that is

Table 6-5
Vocational Programs in Men's and Women's Prisons

MALE PRISONS	Air Cond. Rep.	Arts & Crafts	Auto Body	Auto Mech.	Baking	Barbering	Bookbinding	Brick Masonry	Build. Maint.	Build. Trades	Cabinet Making	Carpentry	Carpet Laying	Chemistry	Computer Maint.	Cooking	Data Proc.	Diving	Drafting	Electronics	Eng. & Appl. Rep.	Farming	Farm Equip.
Frank Lee (Ala.)			x	x		x		x			x									x	x		
Atmore			x					x														x	
Draper			x	x		x		x			x									x	x		
Holman																							
Cal. Corr. (Cal.)	x		x	x							x									x			
Cal. Inst.			x									x					x	x					
Folsom			x	x																x			
San Quentin					x		x												x				
Cheshire (Conn.)			x	x								x											
Osborn			x	x						x						x							
Somers			x													x				x			
Menard (Ill.)					x							x							x				
Pontiac					x	x										x			x	x			
Statesville					x	x				x						x				x			
State Farm (Ind.)					x												x						
State Pris.			x	x	x		x													x			
State Ref.			x	x	x		x												x		x		
Ionia (Mich.)			x																	x			
Jackson			x									x					x	x					
State Pris. (Minn.)			x		x										x		x	x					
State Ref.			x	x	x	x		x		x	x						x	x					
Parchman (Miss.)			x				x	x				x							x				x
Int. Ref. (Mo.)			x	x								x							x				
State Pen.																	x			x	x		
Training Center			x	x															x		x		
Lincoln (Neb.)			x	x						x	x									x			
Clinton (N.Y.)						x																	
Elmira			x	x	x						x								x	x			
Green Haven			x	x							x								x	x			
Wallkill			x	x	x						x									x			
Chillicothe (O.)											x								x	x			
Lebanon	x		x													x							
Marion			x	x				x															
So. O. Cor.																				x			
State Ref.	x		x					x			x								x				
State Cor. (Oreg.)			x	x	x	x		x	x							x				x	x	x	
State Pen.			x	x								x						x		x	x		
Rockview (Pa.)			x		x	x		x				x					x			x		x	x
Camp Hill	x		x	x	x	x		x	x	x	x	x	x			x	x			x	x	x	x
Dallas	x	x	x	x	x			x		x		x	x			x						x	x
Graterford		x	x	x	x						x						x			x		x	x
Huntingdon		x	x	x	x	x	x	x	x	x	x	x	x			x					x	x	x
Pittsburgh	x		x	x	x	x	x	x	x	x	x			x			x						
Reg. Cor.												x											
Monroe (Wash.)			x	x	x	x						x							x	x			
Shelton			x	x	x	x						x		x				x		x	x	x	
Walla Walla			x	x																	x		

Forestry	Furniture Mfr.	Graphics	Horticulture	Laundry	Leather Work	Machine Shop	Meat Cutting	Metal Work	Off. Mach. Rep.	Optics	Painting	Plumbing	Printing	Radio, TV Rep.	Recreation Aid	Silk Screening	Shoe Repair	Steam Fitting	Tailoring	Watch Repair	Welding	Clerical	Cosmetology	Dental Tech.	Floral Design	Food Service	Garment Mfr.	Housekeeping	IBM Keypunch	Nurses' Aide	TOTAL
	x																				x										9
																	x			x	x										5
	x																				x										9
																															0
			x			x	x									x	x				x					x					12
						x		x									x														6
						x	x	x					x																		7
			x			x	x	x	x						x	x	x		x		x			x							13
						x													x					x							6
																				x	x			x							7
																					x										3
	x					x					x			x							x										8
	x		x			x					x										x										9
						x					x										x										5
						x	x														x										6
x						x					x		x		x						x										11
	x					x							x	x	x	x		x			x										17
						x		x						x	x						x										9
						x		x					x	x							x										9
									x												x			x						x	7
						x	x		x										x		x										9
	x					x															x		x								9
																										x					2
						x								x	x		x		x		x										12
						x						x	x														x				9
						x		x				x	x	x		x					x										11
												x																			5
													x	x		x					x	x				x			x		9
													x								x	x									5
														x							x										3
			x											x							x					x	x				10
		x	x						x										x	x										x	15
																					x									x	8
	x			x			x							x	x						x		x	x	x						18
	x	x	x	x	x	x	x	x					x	x	x	x	x		x		x	x		x		x	x	x			39
	x		x	x		x	x	x					x	x					x		x	x	x	x		x	x	x		x	28
x									x								x							x							12
	x			x	x	x	x	x					x	x	x				x		x	x		x	x		x	x		x	34
			x	x	x	x	x							x	x			x	x		x			x			x				24
																												x			2
			x	x		x	x												x												12
			x	x		x	x														x										13
			x													x												x			6

Table 6-5 (continued)

FEMALE PRISONS	Air Cond. Rep.	Arts & Crafts	Auto Body	Auto Mech.	Baking	Barbering	Bookbinding	Brick Masonry	Build. Maint.	Build. Trades	Cabinet Making	Carpentry	Carpet Laying	Chemistry	Computer Maint.	Cooking	Data Proc.	Diving	Drafting	Electronics	Eng. & Appl. Rep.	Farming	Farm Equip.
Tutwiler (Ala.)																							
Cal. Inst. (Cal.)																							
Niantic (Conn.)																							
Dwight (Ill.)																							
Women's Pris. (Ind.)																							
Det. Cor. (Mich.)																							
Women's Pris. (Minn.)																							
Parchman (Miss.)																							
Cor. Cent. (Mo.)																							
York (Neb.)																							
Bedford Hills (N.Y.)																							
Women's Pris. (O.)																							
Women's Cor. (Oreg.)																							
Muncy (Pa.)																							
Purdy (Wash.)																							

Source: Adapted from Ralph R. Arditi, Frederick Goldberg, Jr., Martha M. Hartle, John H. Peters, William R. Phelps, The Sexual Segregation of American Prisons: Notes. 82 Yale Law Journal No. 6. 1229-1273.

characteristic of at least a pre World War II era. Table 6-5 compares the diversity and types of vocational programs available for men and women inmates at forty-seven male and fifteen female institutions. These institutions account for approximately 30 percent of the men and 50 percent of the women inmates in the country.

The average number of programs in the men's prisons is 10; in female institutions the average number is 2.7. Whereas male prisoners have a choice of some fifty different vocational programs, the women's choices are limited to cosmetology (and in some states convicted felons are forbidden by law to work in this field), clerical training, food services, serving, IBM key punching, and nurses' aides. Some of the men's prisons provide vocational training in programs that are available to women inmates as well; but none of the prisons for women are prepared to train their inmates in programs that are available for men.

The industries available at men's and women's institutions that

Forestry	Furniture Mfr.	Graphics	Horticulture	Laundry	Leather Work	Machine Shop	Meat Cutting	Metal Work	Off. Mach. Rep.	Optics	Painting	Plumbing	Printing	Radio, TV Rep.	Recreation Aid	Silk Screening	Shoe Repair	Steam Fitting	Tailoring	Watch Repair	Welding	Clerical	Cosmetology	Dental Tech.	Floral Design	Food Service	Garment Mfr.	Housekeeping	IBM Keypunch	Nurses' Aide	TOTAL
																							X	X	X						3
																							X					X	X		3
																						X							X		2
																						X	X								2
																						X	X								2
																						X		X					X		3
																										X	X		X		3
																													X		1
																						X	X						X		3
																										X	X				2
																								X			X		X		3
																						X	X			X	X		X	X	6
																						X							X		2
																								X					X	X	3
																						X				X			X		3

can provide a source of livelihood for the inmates show much the same picture (table 6-6). In the forty-seven prisons for men there is an average of 3.2 industries as compared to 1.2 in the fifteen female prisons. There is also hardly any overlap concerning the types of industries in which both male and female inmates may work. According to Burkhart (1973, p. 302) prisoners (men and women) are still employed in the personal service of prison administrators. Women prisoners often work as housemaids and cooks for the families of prison superintendents.

Both in the types of work for which the men are being trained after they leave prison, and in the work available to them in prison as a source of income, the opportunities for earning better incomes at a wider variety of jobs gives the male inmates an advantage over the female. Although women are still much less likely to be sent to prison than are men, once there, the opportunities afforded to women for rehabilitation and vocational training are much less than are those for men.

Table 6-6
Industries in Men's and Women's Prisons

MALE PRISONS	Auto Rep.	Bookbindery	Cabinet Making	Cloth Mfr.	Coffee Roasting	Concrete	Dairy	Data Proc.	Dental	Detergent Mfr.	Farming	Flag Mfr.	Furniture Mfr.	Heavy Equip. Op.	Library	License Plate	Machine Shop	Metal Shop	Printing	Road Sign Mfr.	Shoe Mfr.	Engine Rpr.	Tailoring	Twine Mfr.	Upholstery	Wax, Brush Mfr.	Canning	Food Service	Garment Mfr.	IBM Keypunch	Laundry	TOTAL
Frank Lee (Ala.)																																0
Atmore											x																					1
Draper											x																					1
Holman											x					x																2
Cal. Cor. (Cal.)												x	x																			2
Cal. Inst.							x						x	x	x														x			5
Folsom														x													x					2
San Quentin										x				x	x																	3
Cheshire (Conn.)	x															x		x		x												4
Osborn																																0
Somers								x					x			x			x	x									x			6
Menard (Ill.)				x									x									x			x	x			x			6
Pontiac						x																										1
Statesville		x				x	x											x											x			5
State Farm (Ind.)										x	x		x				x												x			5
State Prison												x				x	x	x	x	x												6
State Ref.												x	x					x	x	x			x									6
Ionia (Mich.)																	x	x											x			3
Jackson																x		x			x								x		x	5
State Prison (Minn.)														x		x								x								3
State Ref.																x													x			2

85

Institution												
Parchman (Miss.)												1
Int. Ref. (Mo.)												1
State Pen.												9
Training Center												4
Lincoln (Neb.)												7
Clinton (N.Y.)												2
Elmira												0
Green Haven												2
Wallkill												0
Chillicothe (O.)												4
Lebanon												3
Marion												3
So. O. Corr. Inst.												4
State Ref.												2
State Cor. (Oreg.)												0
State Pen.												5
Rockview (Pa.)												3
Camp Hill												3
Dallas												4
Graterford												7
Huntingdon												5
Pittsburgh												4
Reg. Cor.												0
Monroe (Wash.)												5
Shelton												1
Walla Walla												4

Table 6-6 (continued)

FEMALE PRISONS	Auto Rep.	Bookbindery	Cabinet Making	Cloth Mfr.	Coffee Roasting	Concrete	Dairy	Data Proc.	Dental	Detergent Mfr.	Farming	Flag Mfr.	Furniture Mfr.	Heavy Equip. Op.	Library	License Plate	Machine Shop	Metal Shop	Printing	Road Sign Mfr.	Shoe Mfr.	Engine Rpr.	Tailoring	Twine Mfr.	Upholstery	Wax, Brush Mfr.	Canning	Food Service	Garment Mfr.	IBM Keypunch	Laundry	TOTAL
Tutwiler (Ala.)																											x		x		x	3
Cal. Inst. (Cal.)																													x			1
Niantic (Conn.)																														x		1
Dwight (Ill.)																															x	1
Women's Prison (Ind.)																											x				x	2
Det. Cor. (Mich.)																																0
Women's Prison (Minn.)																													x			1
Parchman (Miss.)																																0
Cor. Center (Mo.)																																0
York (Neb.)																												x				1
Bedford Hills (N.Y.)																												x	x		x	3
Women's Prison (O.)																													x	x		2
Women's Cor. (Oreg.)																																0
Muncy (Pa.)											x																			x		2
Purdy (Wash.)																																0

Source: Adapted from Ralph R. Arditi, Frederick Goldberg, Jr., Martha M. Hartle, John H. Peters, William R. Phelps, The Sexual Segregation of American Prisons: Notes. 82 Yale Law Journal 1229-1273, Appendix III.

7

The Parole System: How Women Fare

All prisoners do not have the same chance of being paroled, and all parolees do not have the same chance of maintaining a successful parole. The likelihood of receiving a favorable parole hearing and of maintaining a successful parole has been shown to be strongly determined by the type of offense for which the prisoner was convicted, the prisoner's prior criminal record, and his or her adjustment and behavior in prison. Other factors considered good predictors are the prisoner's prior history of drug and alcohol use and his or her age at the time of conviction.

Younger offenders are more likely to violate the conditions of their parole than are older offenders. Prisoners with a history of drug or alcohol use are less likely to have successful paroles than are those without such a history. Property offenders have higher rates of parole violations than do prisoners convicted of crimes of violence. The lowest rates of parole violations are associated with prisoners who were convicted of homicide, manslaughter, forcible rape, and aggravated assault; and the highest with auto theft, forgery, larceny, and other types of fraud. The percents in table 7-1 show that the range of favorable or successful parole performances are from 91 for homicide to 57 for auto theft.

From the data in chapters 4 and 5 we know that women are more highly represented in those offenses that have less successful paroles. On the other hand, women prisoners are by and large more passive, quieter, and less likely to riot or engage in other forms of disruptive behavior. Recidivism rates do not appear to differ significantly for men and women. All things considered then, there is no overriding theory that would lead one to expect differences in the parole performance of men and women, once the type of offense for which the prisoner was convicted was controlled.

In the last few years the National Council on Crime and Delinquency Research Center has published an annual newsletter in which they describe parole outcomes for the country as a whole. Fifty-five agencies from each of the states, except Alaska, are rep-

Table 7-1

Type of Offense and Favorable Parole Performance Based on a One-Year Follow-Up of Males and Females Paroled from Twenty-Two Agencies: January - December 1965.

Type of Offense	Parole Favorable (No Major Difficulty)	Performance Unfavorable (Major Difficulty)	Percent Favorable
Homicide	539	54	90.9
Manslaughter	72	12	85.7
Armed Robbery	813	256	76.1
Unarmed Robbery	287	109	72.5
Aggravated Assault	309	62	83.3
Forcible Rape	135	33	80.4
Statutory Rape	87	25	77.7
Sex Offenses against Juveniles	129	24	84.3
Other Sex Offenses	50	15	76.9
Prostitution and Pandering	8	5	72.7
Burglary	1576	796	66.4
Theft or Larceny	504	212	70.4
Vehicle Theft	219	162	57.5
Forgery and Checks	435	317	57.9
Other Fraud	48	12	80.0
Narcotics Violations	256	105	70.9
Alcohol Violations	36	9	80.0
All Others	267	135	66.4
Total	5770	2343	71.1

Source: Adapted from *A National Uniform Parole Reporting System* (Davis, Calif.: National Probation and Parole Institutes, December 1970), table 22, p. 75.

resented, although not all states report on 100 percent of their parolees. The newsletter describes parole outcomes for men and women by the type of offense for which they were committed, their history of drug and alcohol use, and their prior prison sentences. For 1970, all of the states listed 100 percent of their parolees in the *Crime and Delinquency Newsletter* with the following exceptions: Alabama, Indiana, Maryland, Pennsylvania and Wisconsin—25 percent; Michigan—18 percent; New York and Ohio—10 percent.

Table 7-2 summarizes the proportions of men and women who were paroled in 1968, 1969, and 1970 by homogeneous offense categories and describes the proportion of women as opposed to men who were paroled for all offenses combined in each of the three years. Note first that the percentages of women who have been paroled for those years are only slightly larger than the proportion of

Table 7-2
Percentage of Offenders Paroled by Sex and Type of Offense: 1968-70

	1968		1969		1970	
Offense Category	Male	Female	Male	Female	Male	Female
Willful Manslaughter	7	13	7	14	7	14
Negligent Manslaughter	2	4	2	4	1	3
Armed Robbery	11	3	11	4	11	5
Unarmed Robbery	3	2	4	1	4	2
Aggravated Assault	6	5	5	6	6	5
Forcible Rape	2	0	2	0	2	0
Statutory Rape	1	0	1	0	1	0
All Other Sex Offenses	3	1	3	2	2	1
Burglary	29	7	30	6	29	8
Theft or Larceny	9	11	9	12	10	11
Vehicle Theft	5	2	5	1	5	1
Forgery and Fraud	10	26	9	27	9	27
Other Fraud	1	2	1	2	1	1
Drug Law Violations	4	12	5	13	5	15
All Others	7	12	6	7	6	7
Total	100	100	100	100	100	100
	(24,786)	(1720)	(25,563)	(1669)	(25,602)	(1710)
Percent Females Paroled		7		6		7

Source: Adapted from *Uniform Parole Reports* (Davis, Calif.: National Council on Crime and Delinquency Research Center).

women inmates in federal and state prisons (about 5 percent) in those years. Preferential treatment for women does not appear to be a significant factor at the parole hearing stage of the criminal justice system.

When we examine the proportion of men and women who were paroled within the same offense category, we find three offenses for which there are both big differences and a sufficient number of women to make the comparisons worthwhile. Men who were convicted of homicide, forgery and fraud, and violation of narcotic drug laws were less likely to be paroled than were women convicted of those offenses: 7 versus 14 percents, 9 versus 27 percents, and 5 versus 14 percents. For the thirteen other offense categories listed, there are no marked or consistent differences between men and women. Among the men, those who were convicted of burglary were most likely to be paroled; among the women, those who were convicted of fraud and forgery were paroled more than those who were committed for any other offense.

These findings appear curious in light of the fact that offenders in these categories have been among those who have had the least successful parole careers. But it is also true that among male prisoners, burglars comprise the largest single category, except for drug offenders (California data, table 6-4); and for women prisoners, those convicted of forgery and fraud comprise the largest category, save for drug offenders. The decision to parole then must also be affected by the various proportions of prisoners who have been convicted of different types of offenses.

Note that in table 6-4 the ratio of women who were sentenced to prison for forgery and fraud compared to homicide is 2.5 to 1; and the ratio of women who were paroled for forgery and fraud compared to homicide is 2 to 1. Among the men who were sentenced to prison in California for burglary and homicide, the ratio is 2.8 to 1 in favor of burglary. Among those selected for parole the ratio is 4.2 to 1 in favor of burglary.

Thus, numbers alone are not likely to explain the parole decisions in favor of male inmates who have been convicted of burglary. But for women, the size of the available pool of inmates may be a more important factor in determining which inmates are likely to be paroled. For both men and women, drug offenders appeared to be treated as special cases, whose chances of being paroled are much dimmer than are their proportions in the prison population.

Table 7-3 describes the percentage of parolees who maintained successful paroles for one year, by the type of offense for which they were originally committed. (For example, among the almost 1500 men who had been sentenced for homicide and were paroled in 1968, 88 percent maintained successful paroles for one year.) Note first that the over-all percentages of women who maintained successful paroles for at least one year are higher than they are for men in 1968, 75 versus 72 percents, in 1969, 76 versus 74 percents, and in 1970, 77 versus 70 percents.

Within each offense category, save for violations of drug laws, a higher proportion of the women are continued on parole after one year than are the men. The biggest and most consistent differences between men and women occur in the forgery and fraud, and the drug violation categories. In forgery and fraud convictions, women are more successful in staying out of prison, and in drug violations they are less successful.

Table 7-3

Percentage of Offenders Continued on Parole by Sex and Type of Offense: 1968-70[a]

Offense Category	1968		1969		1970	
	Male	Female	Male	Female	Male	Female
Willful Homicide	88	91	89	93	87	92
Negligent Manslaughter	87	88	89	93	89	93
Armed Robbery	74	70	75	71	78	82
Aggravated Assault	76	82	80	77	79	78
Burglary	70	71	71	71	73	72
Theft or Larceny	72	74	72	76	73	74
Forgery and Fraud	64	73	66	71	65	74
Drug Law Violations	73	66	78	68	80	68
All Others	74	68	73	69	75	76
All Offenses	72	75	74·	76	70	77
	(20855)	(1595)	(21654)	(1563)	(21845)	(1609)

[a]Numbers in parentheses denote total number of parolees considered (includes parolees not continued on parole). Some of the offenses included in table 7-2 are not included in table 7-3 because there are too few women in those offense categories.

Source: Adapted from *Uniform Parole Reports* (Davis, Calif.: National Council on Crime and Delinquency Research Center).

When we compared the likelihoods of men and women with drug histories gaining successful parole hearings (table 7-4), we found that more than twice the proportion of women who were paroled had such histories as did men.

But women with drug histories turned out to be the poorer parole risks. They were less likely to remain out of prison than were women who had no history of drug usage or men who also had histories of drug usage (table 7-5).

Table 7-5 suggests that a history of drug usage is a better predictor for how successful women will be in their paroles than men. When there is no history of drug usage, a higher proportion of women maintain successful paroles for at least one year.

We also compared successful paroles between men and women by their histories of prior commitments. As the percentages in table 7-6 show, men and women who had been committed for the first time prior to their parole were much more likely to have successful paroles than were parolees who had at least one prior commitment. There was no difference between the men and women who had no

Table 7-4
Percentage of Men and Women Paroled With History of Drug Usage

	Men	*Women*
1968	12 (23,746)	32 (1,644)
1969	15 (25,472)	34 (1,668)
1970	18 (25,582)	37 (1,710)

prior commitments as to the proportion who stayed out for at least one year. But having served time on at least one prior occasion reduced the likelihood that women would maintain successful paroles more than it did for men. A smaller proportion of the women with prior commitments remained out than did men with prior commitments.

One explanation for this phenomenon might be that men are more rigorously screened than are women at the time of the parole hearing. Women are released in part because of their roles in the larger society; but men must demonstrate that they have been rehabilitated, and that they can support themselves. Another explanation might be that parole officers expect women to adhere to higher standards of behavior than they do men; therefore, women's paroles are likely to be terminated for behavior that would result only in a reprimand for men. Behaving properly and in conformity with society's standards is expected of the female more than it is of the male.

In sum, this chapter has shown that the proportion of women who have been paroled in 1968, 1969, and 1970, about 7 percent, was only slightly higher than the proportion of women inmates in federal and state institutions, about 5 percent. Once paroled, women seem to fare slightly better than men in being able to remain out of prison with two exceptions: those with a history of drug use and those with a history of prior commitments. Women in both of these categories have less successful paroles than do men. Whether it is because society places higher standards on them or because they break the rules of their parole more frequently than do men, we cannot discern from these data.

Table 7-5
Percentage of Offenders Continued on Parole by Sex and History of Drug Use: 1968-70[a]

Drug Use	1968		1969		1970	
	Male	Female	Male	Female	Male	Female
History	64	60	66	61	70	65
	(2961)	(526)	(3891)	(573)	(4688)	(639)
No History	74	81	75	83	76	85
	(20,785)	(1118)	(21,581)	(1095)	(20,894)	(1071)

[a]Number in parentheses denote total number of parolees considered (includes parolees not continued on parole).

Source: Adapted from *Uniform Parole Reports* (Davis, Calif.: National Council on Crime and Delinquency Research Center).

Table 7-6
Percentage of Parolees Continued on Parole by Sex and Prior Prison Term: 1968-70[a]

Prior Prison Terms	1968		1969		1970	
	Male	Female	Male	Female	Male	Female
None	77	78	78	78	79	79
	(15,160)	(1311)	(16,395)	(1366)	(17,062)	(1401)
One	68	60	71	66	72	68
	(4578)	(228)	(4881)	(221)	(4519)	(215)
Two or More	64	50	64	60	65	67
	(2087)	(105)	(4287)	(82)	(4021)	(94)

[a]Numbers in parentheses denote all parolees considered (includes parolees not continued on parole).

Source: Adapted from *Uniform Parole Reports* (Davis, Calif.: National Council on Crime and Delinquency Research Center).

8

The British Scene: A Brief Review

The United States has not been the only country to experience a women's liberation movement in recent years. Other industrialized countries with developed economies have also witnessed the resurgence of a feminist movement, the major goals of which have also been equal employment opportunities, the repeal of discriminatory legislation, and demands for greater political participation and representation.

In Britain, as in the United States, experts in societal processes and mental health have anticipated and, indeed, have asserted that a relationship exists between women's demands for equal treatment in the law abiding and conformist spheres of society and an increase in women's tendency to engage in law-breaking deviant behavior.

In the summer of 1973, the *London Times* devoted a three-column spread to the topic "Crime and Femininity."

Everyone I spoke to last week in person, in the courts, and in the probation service confirmed that female crime and particularly offenses of violence is increasing at a faster rate than male crime. Home office figures also point to the same conclusion. Trevor Gibbons, Professor of Psychiatry, echoes the thought of many involved in female crime when he says that the general emancipation of women is one factor in their increased criminality.

British criminal statistics are much more useful for research purposes than are those regularly published anywhere in the United States. Each year in Great Britain, it is possible to obtain information from published data describing the sex and age of the number of persons apprehended and proceeded against for each category of offense. In addition, conviction rates, and types of sentences are analyzed by offense category, age, and sex.

Table 8-1 describes the proportion of women who were convicted in England and Wales of any indictable offense in 1950, the early sixties, and from 1968 through 1971. Note that twenty years earlier one out of 7.7, or 13 percent, of those convicted was a woman; and in 1971, slightly more than one out of 7.2, or 13.8

Table 8-1
Percentages of Persons Found Guilty of Indictable Offenses: Distribution among Age and Sex Groups in England and Wales: 1950, 1960-63, 1968-71

Age Group	1950 Male	1950 Female	1960 Male	1960 Female	1961 Male	1961 Female	1962 Male	1962 Female	1963 Male	1963 Female
Under 14	21.1	1.5	16.9	1.4	16.4	1.6	14.2	1.5	13.0	1.3
14 to 16	12.6	1.3	15.1	1.6	15.5	1.8	15.0	1.8	15.9	1.8
17 to 20	9.4	1.5	15.3	1.7	15.2	1.7	15.6	1.7	16.2	1.7
21 to 29	18.9	2.6	19.7	2.0	19.6	2.2	20.4	2.3	20.7	2.3
30 and over	25.0	6.1	21.0	5.3	20.4	5.6	21.2	6.3	21.2	5.9
All Ages	87.0	13.0	88.0	12.0	87.1	12.9	86.4	13.6	87.0	13.0

Age Group	1968 Male	1968 Female	1969 Male	1969 Female	1970 Male	1970 Female	1971 Male	1971 Female
Under 14	8.6	1.0	7.3	0.8	6.6	0.8	5.6	0.5
14 to 16	13.6	1.8	14.1	1.6	14.0	1.7	13.7	1.6
17 to 20	19.9	2.1	21.7	2.1	21.6	2.2	22.1	2.5
21 to 29	23.2	2.9	23.6	3.0	23.7	3.1	23.4	3.4
30 and over	21.2	5.7	20.3	5.5	20.9	5.4	21.4	5.8
All Ages	86.5	13.5	87.0	13.0	86.8	13.2	86.2	13.8

Source: Adapted from Criminal Statistics, England and Wales. Presented to Parliament by the Secretary of State for the Home Department by Command of Her Majesty, July, 1961, 1964, 1969, 1970, 1971 (London: Her Majesty's Stationery Office).

percent, of those convicted was a woman. Such changes are negligible.

When men and women are divided into homogeneous age categories, we see that from 1968 onward, more men in the twenty-one-to-thirty category have been convicted than in the over-thirty category. Among women there has been a shift in that direction, but as of 1971, most of the women convicted are still in the over-thirty category. The male-to-female ratio of conviction rates in California is slightly higher than it is in Britain. In California, during the same time period, approximately one out of nine persons convicted was a woman.

According to the *London Times* (Watson, July 22, 1973) women in Britain today are committing more crimes of violence than they have in the recent past. But an examination of the percentages in table 8-2 shows that there has been no sizable increase in the past two decades. In 1950, the ratio was one woman for every twelve men; in 1960 the ratio was one woman for every twenty-two men, and in 1970 the ratio was one woman for every seventeen men.

When the conviction rates are broken by age, we see that there has been an increase in the proportion of girls under seventeen who have been convicted of violent crimes but not among women in any of the other age categories.

The 5.8 percent female conviction rate in 1971 for crimes of violence in Britain is about 60 percent of that reported in California for female homicide and assault rates in those same years.

As in the United States, the crimes in Britain for which women account for the highest proportion of convictions are theft (20 percent in 1971) and fraud (15 percent in 1971). But the data in table 8-3 do not show that the proportion of female convictions for theft has increased over the past decade. Again as in the United States, women make up only a tiny proportion of the burglary and robbery convictions, about 2.5 percent.

The data describing the proportion of British women in prison also have strong similarities to the United States, as shown by the percentages in table 8-4. For example, the proportion of women who have been incarcerated has declined from 6 percent in 1937 to 2 percent in 1968. The same downward trend is shown in the data for the United States.

But the impression held in the United States that women prisoners are more docile and less troublesome does not seem to be

Table 8-2
Number of Men and Women and the Percentage of Females Found Guilty of Violence Against the Person, by Age and Sex, in England and Wales, 1950, 1960-71[a]

Year	Under 17		17-20		21-29		30 and Over		All Ages	
	N	% Female	N	% Female	N	% Female	N	% Female	N	% Female
1950	315	1.3	468	4.5	1577	6.8	1479	12.4	3,839	8.0
1960	1583	2.7	2762	1.8	3421	3.8	2493	9.7	10,259	4.5
1961	1717	2.4	3006	2.2	3909	5.0	2887	8.5	11,519	4.3
1962	1787	2.4	3293	2.9	3993	4.8	2913	9.2	11,986	5.0
1963	1896	3.0	3463	2.8	4361	4.6	3112	8.7	12,832	4.8
1964	1978	3.6	3985	2.1	4729	4.7	3449	9.4	14,141	5.0
1965	2004	5.8	4495	2.4	5238	5.1	3764	8.8	15,501	5.3
1966	1793	7.1	4616	2.6	5530	5.5	4097	8.1	16,036	5.5
1967	1840	6.6	4849	2.5	5681	5.1	4706	7.9	17,076	5.3
1968	1882	7.7	5051	2.4	6330	5.4	5075	8.3	18,338	5.6
1969	2249	10.8	5742	2.6	7157	4.8	5707	7.7	20,855	5.4
1970	2827	12.6	6298	3.7	7963	5.0	6355	7.4	22,443	5.8
1971	3574	13.6	6927	4.0	8698	5.0	7067	7.0	26,266	5.8

[a]The number includes men and women.

Source: Adapted from *Criminal Statistics, England and Wales*. Presented to Parliament by the Secretary of State for the Home Department by Command of Her Majesty, July, 1961, 1964, 1969, 1970, 1971 (London: Her Majesty's Stationery Office).

Table 8-3

Number of Men and Women and the Percentage of Females Found Guilty of Theft, by Sex, in England and Wales: 1950, 1960-71[a]

Year	Number	Percent Female
1950	73,219	16
1960	96,398	16
1961	107,235	18
1962	119,034	19
1963	120,384	19
1964	119,266	20
1965	128,615	20
1966	135,611	19
1967	141,411	19
1968	147,009	19
1969	167,440	18
1970	176,502	18
1971	171,629	20

[a]The number includes men and women.

Source: Adapted from *Criminal Statistics, England and Wales*. Presented to Parliament by the Secretary of State for the Home Department by Command of Her Majesty, July, 1961, 1964, 1969, 1970, 1971 (London: Her Majesty's Stationery Office).

Table 8-4

Prisoners by Sex in England and Wales: 1938, 1948, 1958, 1963 and 1968

Year	Total	Male	Female	Percent Female
1938	8,926	8,368	558	6
1948	16,659	15,736	923	5
1958	21,209	20,474	735	3
1963	24,966	24,156	810	3
1968	25,320	24,712	608	2

Source: Adapted from *People in Prison, England and Wales*. Presented to Parliament by the Secretary of State for the Home Department by Command of Her Majesty, November 1969.

supported by the data from British prisons. On the one hand, for four out of the five years shown in table 8-5 a smaller proportion of the female inmates were punished than were the males; but on the other hand, the average numbers of offenses committed per inmate was consistently higher for the female prisoners than it was for the males. When we compared the types of offenses for which inmates were

Table 8-5

Percentage of Inmates Punished, by Sex, in England and Wales: 1959-63

Year	Total Males	Annual No. of Offenses Per Head of Average Population	Percent of Males Punished	Total Females	Annual No. of Offenses Per Head of Average Population	Percent of Females Punished
1959	16,113	0.8	55	588	.9	49
1960	16,589	0.8	63	565	1.1	39
1961	18,130	0.9	56	573	1.3	51
1962	19,471	0.8	60	615	1.5	79
1963	18,859	0.7	63	545	1.1	51

Source: Adapted from *Prisons and Borstals 1963*. Presented to Parliament by the Secretary of State for the Home Department by Command of Her Majesty, June 1964.

Table 8-6

Types of Offenses and Percentages of Inmates Punished, by Sex, in England and Wales: 1959-63

Year	Violence Against the Person		Offenses Damage to Property		Idleness		Other Offenses	
	Percent Male	Percent Female	Percent Male	Percent Female	Percent Male	Percent Female	Percent Male	Percent Female
1959	4	7	7	12	6	3	81	77
1960	4	9	7	13	6	3	81	74
1961	3	6	7	17	6	6	82	70
1962	3	2	6	22	6	4	83	70
1963	3	2	6	16	6	3	83	77

Source: Adapted from *Prisons and Borstals 1963*. Presented to Parliament by the Secretary of State for the Home Department by Command of Her Majesty, June 1964.

punished, we found that women were more likely to commit and be punished for offenses against property than were men, a pattern that is found outside the prison as well (table 8-6).

The opportunities for occupational training and employment for women in British prisons appear to be no better and just as sex-biased as they are for men. Of the 632 women in prisons in Britain in 1963 who were certified as fit for labor, 55 percent were employed in domestic service (that is, as cooks and bakers, laundry workers, cleaners) compared to 28 percent of the 21,080 men inmates in the

Table 8-7

Employment in Men's and Women's Prisons in England and Wales: 1963

Employment	Males	Females
Manufactures:		
Basketmakers	26	
Blacksmiths	79	
Bookbinders	225	
Brush and mop making	144	
Carpenters	412	
Concrete molders	21	
Fitters	99	
Heavy canvaswork, other than mailbags	400	
Jam making	—	13
Knitters and repairers	180	9
Mailbags (new)	2779	11
Mailbags repairers	833	
Mats, matting and rugs	495	
Mattresses (coir and hair)	306	
Metal recovery	1301	
Molders (iron foundry)	24	
Needleworkers, dressmakers, and repairers	112	101
Netmakers	159	
Pouch and leatherwork	162	
Printers	72	
Ship fenders	25	
Shoemakers and repairers	393	
Storemen	118	
Tagmakers	328	
Tailors and repairers	1278	2
Tinsmiths	86	
Toy assembly and painting	418	41
Tubular steel furniture makers	29	
Twine and ropemakers	17	
Weavers: cotton, linen and woolen	306	
Wire fencing	—	
Woodchopping	169	
Miscellaneous[a]	509	28
	11,504	205
Farm:		
Livestock and arable husbandry, market gardening, glass, land reclamation	781	17
Works Department:		
Bricklayers and masons	255	1
Carpenters and joiners	174	1
Electricians	92	1
Fitters	109	
Laborers	805	3

Table 8-7 (continued)

Employment	Males	Females
Painters and decorators	388	17
Plasterers	43	
Plumbers	111	
Quarrymen	37	
Slaters	2	
Total	2,015	23
Domestic service:		
Cleaners, jobbers and laborers	3,729	177
Cooks and bakers	907	54
Gardeners	590	31
Hospital orderlies	140	16
Laundry workers	559	70
Stokers	112	
Total	6,037	348
Outside work:		
For farmers, private firms and local authorities	202	
For government departments	203	
Total	405	
Vocational trainees	620	18
Pre-release hostellers	123	21
Total effectives	743	39
Noneffectives:		
Untried prisoners who elect not to work	782	25
Certified unfit for labor	190	23
Sick	748	103
Under punishment	145	2
Others[b]	802	20
Total	2,667	173
Grand Total	23,747	805

[a]Includes sorting, salvage, and simple assembly.

[b]Including inmates who are noneffective as a working unit on day of discharge. Travelling between establishments. Attending court. At summer camp.

Source: Adapted from *Prisons and Borstals 1963*. Presented to Parliament by the Secretary of State for the Home Department by Command of Her Majesty, June 1964.

same year who were also so certified. Fifty-three percent of the male inmates were employed in manufactures (bookbinding, carpentry, making mailbags, metal recovery, etc.) compared to 32 percent of the women inmates. But even among those women who did work in "manufactures," half worked as dressmakers and repairers. It is interesting that the same small proportion of men and women, 4 percent, elected not to work. A detailed description of the relative employment opportunities for male and female inmates in 1963 in British prisons is provided in table 8-7.

In summary, the British scene has many similarities with the American. For example, the belief that women's participation in crime, especially crimes of violence, has increased, is much greater than the data substantiate. Women in England, as in the United States, are more likely to engage in theft and fraud than they are in crimes of violence. As in the United States, there has also been a decline in the percentage of women in Britain who have been committed to prison over the past three decades. But perhaps, unlike in the United States, women prisoners in England may be more troublesome and receive more punishments. Finally, women prisoners in England seem to be subjected to "sex-typed employment" and to limitations in employment and vocational opportunities to much the same degree that they are in the United States. The British data on female employment in prisons are eight years older than are those shown for the United States, so there is at least some hope that improvements have been made.

9

Summary and Conclusions: A Look to the Future

We have learned that female criminality has received much less attention by criminologists, law enforcement officials, and community and clinical psychologists than has male criminality. Even the most recent texts in criminology either ignore the topic, mention it in passing, or devote at most only a few pages to it.

Most people who have written on the topic usually adopt one of two positions, which they cling to with great tenacity. One group perceives women who commit crimes as poor benighted victims of male oppression and of society's indifference. The other group perceives women offenders as being more cunning and more crafty than men, as having learned how to commit crimes that are more difficult to apprehend, and as believing that they can count on the chivalry of male law enforcement officials to avoid arrest, conviction, and imprisonment.

Those who have adopted the first position do not argue with what the official statistics show about the prevalence of women in crime, that women account for only a small proportion of all crimes and that they are generally underrepresented given their proportion in the population. But those who have adopted the second position assert that the statistics distort rather than describe the real picture of the amount of crime that women commit. They argue that if male victims, police, prosecutors, and judges would forgo their chivalrous behavior, the proportion of women arrested and convicted would be vastly increased.

The position that leaders of the women's movement have taken on this issue seems to fall in between these two perspectives. The leaders of the women's movement claim that women are prepared to lose or to give up whatever preferential treatment the double standard has allowed them. Some of the women who are at the helm of the women's movement are prepared to trade protective labor laws, for equal job opportunities and equal just as they are prepared to trade preferential and paternalistic treatment at the hands of law enforcement officials for due process in civil and criminal procedures. The women's movement also claims that women are no more moral, or conforming, or law-abiding than are men; and that women should neither bask in their superiority over men nor feel they are trapped into wearing a mask of morality and goodness.

If one of the consequences of sexual equality should turn out to be higher crime rates among women, the women's movement would not feel that it has all been in vain. The contemporary leadership might then do what the leaderships of earlier women's movements have done after their immediate goals were realized: turn their efforts and energies to treating other important social ills that affect both men and women.

In the few years since the contemporary women's movement has crystallized as a social movement distinct and independent of either the civil rights or the New Left movements, it has attracted a good deal of attention. It would be reasonable to assume, therefore, that it has had some effect on the psyche, the consciousness, and the self-perceptions of many women in American society. But the extent to which it has motivated those women to act outside the law in order to gain financial rewards, vengeance, and/or power is still too early to say.

In our review of the demographic data, we found that proportionally there are more women in the labor force today than there have ever been in American history (during periods of peace) and that married women with children are holding full-time jobs in higher proportions than ever before. A higher proportion of women are also attending college than have in the past.

But when women's participation in the labor force was examined in more detail, we found that there has not been a big increase in the proportion of women who are employed in the higher-status occupations. Indeed, higher proportions of women today are represented in the traditionally female occupations than at any previous time. Before women's contributions to crime can be expected to match their representation in society, women must have the opportunities for committing those crimes. Those opportunities will come primarily through their positions in the labor force. It is not enough that almost half of all the women work; they must also have those types of jobs that will provide them with the opportunities to commit offenses that are important enough to report. Even if we assume that women's psyche and motivations are no different than men's in their willingness to commit crimes, unless their opportunities expand, it is unlikely that women's crime rates will show a big increase.

Although some law enforcement officials may be moved to give women the equality some say they want, out of respect for the rhetoric of the women's movement, they are much more likely to do so if police, prosecutors, and judges are confronted with much greater numbers of women accused of defrauding, embezzling, and stealing significant amounts of money and property.

What the statistics show about the proportion of women in crime in 1972 are that there are more women involved today than there has been at any time since the end of World War II, and probably before that. But the increase has been in certain types of offenses; theft, forgery, fraud, and embezzlement, not in crimes of violence or in the traditional female crimes, such as prostitution and child abuse.

As of 1972, 30 percent of all arrests for major larceny were women; 30 percent of all the arrests for fraud and embezzlement were women; and 25 percent of all forgery arrests were women. These proportions are not 50 percent, but they are at least twice as high as they are for any other offenses; and if present trends continue, in twenty years women should be making a contribution in white-collar, financial crimes commensurate with their representation in the society. The fact that female arrests have increased for these offenses and not for all offenses is consistent both with opportunity theory and with the presence of a sizable women's movement.

Unfortunately, judicial statistics are not available in a form that permit long-range analysis. The federal statistics, for whatever they are worth, show that there has been an increase in the proportion of women who have been convicted for white-collar offenses from 1963 to the present time. They are useful, at least, in that they are consistent with the arrest data.

But the California data on the proportion of women convicted between 1960 and 1972 do not show that the increase in convictions has followed the increase in arrests for the same type of offenses. Although there has been an increase of 31 percent in the proportion of women convicted for all types of crimes from 1962 to 1972, that increase was due solely to the higher conviction rates for violent offenses.

A comparison of the likelihood of a man being convicted for a given offense over that of a woman shows that for every twelve men convicted, there will be ten women. Men are more likely to be found guilty of murder and robbery than are women. Women also stand a better chance of gaining acquittals for theft and forgery than do men; but on drug charges, there is little difference.

The prison statistics, which extend back over two decades, do not show a growing proportion of women being sentenced. Rather, a better case can be made for the opposite course. When decisions about whether to grant paroles are considered, women do not appear to have any great advantages. Once parole is granted, however, they are somewhat more likely than men to stay out. The two types of exceptions are women with prior commitments and women with a history of drug usage.

In sum, the picture today about how women fare at various stages in the criminal justice system is that although one in 6.5 arrests are women and one in nine convictions are women, only about one in thirty of those sentenced to prison are women. These ratios have not changed drastically over the past two decades, even though these years have seen a women's movement develop and expand, and an increase in the proportion of women working full time outside their homes.

It is time now to shift the focus to the future to try to make some projections about how women's participation in crime will affect their treatment at the hands of law enforcement officials. As part of our effort to find out what the future holds for women offenders, we interviewed about thirty criminal trial court judges and states attorneys in four large cities in the Midwest: Chicago, St. Louis, Milwaukee, and Indianapolis. The interviews asked these experts in law enforcement to describe their experiences with female offenders; more specifically, to characterize the types of offenses with which women are usually charged, the personal and socioeconomic characteristics of those women, and to explain whether they treat female defendants differently than they do male defendants. In addition, we asked whether they have observed changes in the number and types of women who appear in their courtroom today in contrast to five or six years ago: differences in the types of offenses with which the women are charged, their roles in those offenses, their demeanor, and their personal and socioeconomic characteristics.

In the last part of the interview we asked our respondents to think ahead several years and to tell us whether they expected any changes in the number and types of women who were likely to appear in their courtroom, changes in the types of offenses for which they would be charged, changes in the roles that they would be likely to perform during the criminal acts, changes in their demeanor, personal appearances, and social characteristics. Finally, we asked whether they thought they would treat women defendants differently in the future than they have in the past or the present.

The profile that we are able to draw of the women whom these officials see most often are that of black, lower-class, poorly educated women with several children. The crimes with which they are charged most often are shoplifting and other forms of theft, drug use, and crimes of passion that involve killing a husband, a lover, or the other woman. Both the judges and the states attorneys emphasized that women tend not to be the managers, organizers, or planners of most of the crimes with which they are involved. They do not see nor do they expect to see any Ma Barkers or her equivalent in their courtrooms. Most often the women are accomplices who get involved because of their commitment to a boyfriend or a husband. In drugs, they tend to be the users, rarely the pushers, and not at all the organizers. Women are also not connected with organized crime.

When asked about their treatment of women, more than half of the judges said that they do treat women more leniently and more gently than they do men; that they are more inclined to recommend probation rather than imprisonment; and if they sentence a woman, it is usually for a shorter time than if the crime had been committed by a man. Only a small proportion of the judges said that they were less likely to convict the women. The point at which they differentiate in favor of the women is at the time of passing sentence. The statistics describing the proportion of women at the arrest, conviction, and sentencing stages support the judges' observations.

Practically none of the respondents thought that they were seeing more women in the courtroom today, or that the women they were seeing were different today from the women they had seen five or six years ago, with the exception that more women of all classes were coming in as drug-users.

As far as the future is concerned, most of the respondents did not anticipate any real difference in the numbers or types of women they would see, in the types of offenses with which they would be charged, in the roles they would play, in their demeanor in the courtroom, or in the respondents' treatment of the women. Most of the respondents still expected that they would be easier on the women when it came to passing sentence. The quarter or so who did anticipate differences thought that more women would be involved in financial or white-collar crimes than in the past, because more women would be in the labor force and, therefore, would have more opportunities to embezzle and defraud. Only three of the respondents mentioned the women's movement as a possible source of influence. Those who did felt that the women's liberation movement gave women a greater sense of independence and a belief that they could do anything that a man could do. If men can commit all types of crimes, so can women.

Appendix
A Comparative Perspective

This appendix compares female arrest rates in major offense categories for about twenty-five countries from the early part of the 1960s to 1970. The aims are to assess on as large a canvas as the data allow the visibility of women in different types of crimes in different societies, to determine whether female visibility in crime has increased, and whether it has increased for certain types of offenses in different societies. For example, are women more likely to be arrested for property and white-collar offenses in the technologically and economically more advanced societies of Western Europe in which presumably they comprise a larger portion of the commercial labor force than they are in the more traditional societies of Africa and Asia? And are women in the latter societies more likely to be apprehended for crimes of violence, the targets of which are usually relatives or persons to whom they feel bound?

For the United States, the expectation was that female arrest rates would have increased over the past decade or so, and that their increase would be especially marked in financial and white-collar offenses. What about other societies? Should female arrest rates in the nations of Western Europe also be expected to increase from 1963 to 1970 for essentially the same reasons? In summary, then, what is being compared in this appendix are the proportion of female arrest rates for different types of crimes across societies that differ in their economic development, their political ideology, and their religious and social values.

The data are taken from the *International Crime Statistics* collected and published by the International Criminal Police Organization. Each volume contains the number of offenses and the number of offenders known to the police per year, the number of cases solved by the police during the given year, and the types of crimes for which offenders have been arrested. The offenders are classified by sex and by whether they are juveniles or adults. The offenses "cover broad categories of ordinary law crimes which are recognized and punished in the criminal law of almost all countries" (*International Crime Statistics 1965-1966*, p. ix). The editors emphasize the limitations in the usefulness of the data by commenting:

Our statistics cannot take into account the different definitions of what

111

constitutes an indictable offense in the various national legislatures. Nor of any changes in legal definitions, the structure of the various services engaged in criminal investigation and the conditions under which it is carried out, which may have occurred during the period covered by the report. Bearing in mind all these unknown factors, together with others which influence the results of police investigation. The figures which appear in this report must be considered approximate and should be interpreted with great caution.

Specifically, the categories are:

1. Murder: any act performed with the purpose of taking human life, no matter in what circumstances. This definition excludes manslaughter and abortion, but not infanticide;

2. Sex offenses: each country uses the definitions of its own laws for determining whether or not an act is a sex crime; rape and trafficking in women are always included;

3. Larceny: any act of intentionally and unlawfully removing property belonging to another person. This category includes such a wide variety of offenses that it was subdivided into major larceny: robbery with dangerous aggravating circumstances (armed robbery, burglary, housebreaking); and minor larceny: all other kinds of larceny (theft, receiving stolen goods);

4. Fraud: any act of gaining unlawful possession of another person's property other than by larceny (i.e., embezzlement, misappropriation, forgery, false pretenses, trickery, deliberate misrepresentation, swindle in general);

5. Counterfeit currency offenses: any violation in connection with manufacture, issuing, altering, smuggling, or traffic in counterfeit currency;

6. Drug offenses: any violation involving illicit manufacture, traffic, transportation, use, etc. of narcotic drugs; and

7. Total number of offenses: the total number of criminal offenses discovered by and reported to the police in the crime statistics of each country. This figure in this category may be greater than the sum of the other categories.

Two ratios have been computed for each country: the number of offenses reported per 100,000 population (this ratio provides a rough measure of the annual crime rate); and the number of detected offenders per 100,000 population (this ratio is equivalent to the arrest rate).

Table A-1 ranks from highest to lowest the twenty-five countries

Table A-1
Volume of Crime for Selected Countries: 1963, 1968, and 1970

Country	1963	1968	1970	Mean
West Indies	11618	8923	9318	9953
Canada	4063	4796	6831	5230
New Zealand	4434	5448	5804	5229
Finland	2382	5145	5771	4433
Israel	2989	3565	4485	3680
Austria	3327	3779	3863	3656
West Germany	2914	3588	3924	3475
Japan	6710	1899	1401	3337
Monaco	2010	3530	3257	2932
Scotland	2567	2933	3042	2847
Fiji	2562	2379	3461	2801
England and Wales	2253	2578	3176	2669
Thailand	2333	2283	2033	2216
Korea	878	2968	2725	2190
France	1599	2356	2251	2069
Bruni	638	2362	2792	1931
Luxembourg	1645	2097	1844	1862
Netherlands	1212	1673	2013	1633
Jamaica	1597	1559	1720	1625
Tanzania	1107	1182	1267	1185
Hong Kong	905	1024	1057	995
Ireland	579	825	1068	824
Tunisia	776	748	733	752
Malawi	551	658	871	693
Cyprus	930	443	380	584

Source: Adapted from *International Crime Statistics,* International Criminal Police Organization (Interpol), 92-Saint Cloud, 1963-64; 1967-68; 1969-70.

for which there are crime rates for the three time periods. A quick perusal of columns one, two, and three shows that the relative rankings for each year have not changed much, and that the average rate is a good summary statistic for each of the years. The countries that appear in the first ten ranks are on the whole more technologically and economically advanced than are those that appear in the bottom ten rankings. But the country with the highest combined ranking is closer economically, technologically, and socially to the bottom-ranked countries. Most of the countries show that there has been an increase in the over-all volume of crime from 1963 to 1970.

Table A-2 ranks those same countries from highest to lowest by the rate of detected offenders or arrest rates per 100,000 population. Since these rates may tell us more about the relative efficiency of the police in those societies than they add to our knowledge about the

Table A-2

Coefficient of Offenders for Selected Countries, 1963, 1968 and 1970, Ranked in Descending Order According to the Mean.

Country	1963	1968	1970	Mean	Rank for Volume of Crime
West Indies	11537	1392	1940	4956	1
Finland	1512	3519	3902	2978	4
Austria	2637	2741	2789	2772	6
Japan	5719	1084	531	2445	8
Fiji	2307	2142	2573	2341	11
Israel	2304	2258	2354	2305	5
New Zealand	752	2964	3162	2293	3
Thailand	2544	2232	2033	2270	13
Korea	753	2924	2806	2161	14
Canada	1309	2684	1412	1802	2
Monaco	1155	1844	1681	1560	9
West Germany	1414	1528	1552	1498	7
Luxembourg	1249	1667	1524	1480	17
Jamaica	610	1567	1638	1272	19
France	909	1238	1076	1074	15
Netherlands	669	797	848	771	18
Tunisia	785	832	623	747	23
Scotland	637	753	831	740	10
Hong Kong	574	639	683	632	21
Tanzania	691	558	538	596	20
England and Wales	433	552	659	548	12
Cyprus	567	319	324	403	25
Malawi	234	319	433	329	24
Ireland	288	334	354	325	22
Bruni	94	248	311	218	16

Source: Adapted from *International Crime Statistics,* International Criminal Police Organization (Interpol), 92-Saint Cloud, 1963-64; 1967-68; 1969-70.

amount of crime in the country, we must first determine how closely the crimes that are known to the police and the crimes that are cleared by arrest correlate with each other in order to decide how much value to place on the arrest statistics reported by those countries. If it turns out that there is little relationship between crimes known to the police and crimes for which persons have been arrested, then the arrest data can be of little value in measuring the amount of female participation in crime.

It turns out that the two rankings are correlated at .85; the correlation thus accounts for 72 percent of the variance. We can assume then that those countries that have high crime rates also have high arrest rates.

The next question is: What is the strength of the relationship between societies that have high crime rates and societies that have high arrest rates for *women*? Are high crime rates good indicators of how extensively women are likely to participate in the criminal activities of a given society? We ran correlations between: (1) the mean volume of crime for the three time periods and the mean proportion of women arrested in the three time periods for all crimes combined; and (2) the mean volume of crimes and the mean proportion of women arrested in specific offense categories: murder, major larceny, minor larceny, and fraud. (We deleted drug violations because there were too few countries that had data for the three time periods.) All correlations are Spearman rank order correlations except for the correlation between volume of crime and coefficient of offenders, which is a Pearson "$\rho - \mu$" correlation. The correlations looked like this:

Crime rates and female arrest rates for *all crimes combined:*   r= .41

Crime rates and female arrest rates for *murder*:   r= .16

Crime rates and female arrest rates for *major larceny:*   r= .30

Crime rates and female arrest rates for *minor larceny*:   r= .41

Crime rates and female arrest rates for *fraud*:   r= .55

Only the correlation between crime rates and female arrests for fraud turned out to be significant at the .01 level. Thus, neither the over-all female arrest rate or the female arrest rate for each of the specific offense categories would be a useful indicator of the amount of crime committed in a given society.

As could have been anticipated, neither is the over-all arrest rate for men and women a good indicator of the proportion of *women* who are likely to be arrested for all crimes combined or for specific offense categories. The correlations look like this:

Arrest rates and female arrest rates for *all crimes combined:*   r= .36

Arrest rates and female arrest rates for *murder*:   r= .13

Arrest rates and female arrest rates for *major larceny:*   r= .25

Arrest rates and female arrest rates for *minor larceny*:   r= .26

Arrest rates and female arrest rates for *fraud*:   r= .27

Table A-3
Rankings of Countries by Percentage of Females Arrested for Various Crimes[a]

Country	Volume of Crime Rank	Coefficient of Offenders Rank	All Crimes Rank	All Crimes Percent	Murder Rank	Murder Percent	Major Larceny Rank	Major Larceny Percent	Minor Larceny Rank	Minor Larceny Percent	Fraud Rank	Fraud Percent	Drugs Rank	Drugs Percent
West Indies	1	1	1	(28.9)	10	(13.3)	11	(3.4)	10	(16.3)	4.5	(15.4)	5	(14.2)
New Zealand	3	7	2	(25.3)	4	(16.9)	6	(4.2)	5	(19.6)	4.5	(15.4)	10	(4.6)
Thailand	13	8	3	(17.3)	18	(4.2)	13	(3.0)	13	(14.4)	12	(10.1)	3	(14.6)
West Germany	7	12	4	(16.4)	9	(15.0)	8	(3.8)	1	(25.5)	1	(21.8)		
Luxembourg	17	13	5	(16.2)			2.5	(8.7)	12	(15.4)	13	(9.5)		
Austria	6	3	6.5	(13.8)	3	(22.0)	2.5	(8.7)	3	(22.6)	2	(20.8)	4	(14.3)
France	15	14	6.5	(13.8)	11	(12.8)	1	(8.8)	7	(16.6)	3	(18.7)		
England and Wales	12	9	8	(13.5)										
Tunisia	22	20	9	(12.8)	6	(15.4)	14	(2.6)	6	(18.5)	7	(14.4)	11	(3.5)
Israel	5	16	10	(12.1)	1	(27.0)	4	(8.5)	17	(7.3)	19	(4.6)	7	(7.7)
Korea	14	6	11	(11.5)	21	(2.8)	15	(2.5)	18	(6.8)	16	(6.6)	2	(23.1)
Scotland	10	19	12	(10.9)	2	(22.4)	7	(4.0)	15	(10.0)	14	(8.2)		
Netherlands	18	17	13	(10.4)	8	(13.4)	9	(3.7)	8.5	(16.6)	6	(14.5)		
Ireland	21	15	14	(10.1)	14	(8.1)	11	(3.4)	2	(23.5)	8	(13.1)		
Monaco	9	23	15	(7.5)	12	(12.5)	16.5	(6.5)	8.5	(16.5)	10	(10.6)		
Tanzania	19	11	16	(6.9)	7	(14.1)	18	(2.2)	20	(4.2)	20	(2.1)		
Cyprus	24	21	17	(6.7)	16	(6.5)	16.5	(2.4)	16	(7.7)	18	(4.7)	8	(6.8)
Finland	4	2	18	(6.6)	15	(6.9)	11	(3.4)	11	(15.9)	11	(10.3)		
Japan	8	4	19	(4.6)	5	(16.5)	19	(1.2)	4	(20.5)	15	(7.0)	1	(24.1)
Malawi	23	22	20	(4.2)	19.5	(4.0)	21	(0.9)	22	(2.6)	21	(1.7)	13	(1.0)
Hong Kong	20	18	21	(3.0)	19.5	(4.0)	20	(1.0)	21	(4.1)	17	(5.5)	12	(2.2)
Fiji	11	5	22.5	(1.9)	16	(4.5)	22	(0.3)	19	(5.1)	22	(0.8)	9	(4.8)
Bruni	16	24	22.5	(1.9)										
Canada	2	10			13	(10.0)	5	(5.5)	14	(13.4)	9	(11.8)	6	(13.9)

[a]All rankings except those for volume of crime and coefficient of offenders are by percentage of females arrested. Rankings for volume of crime and coefficient of offenders are for both male and female crimes. Figures in parentheses denote percentage of females among all arrests for that specified crime, averaged over 1963, 1968, and 1970. Blanks appear in the table because figures for those cells were incomplete or not available.

Source: Adapted from International Crime Statistics, International Criminal Police Organization (Interpol), 92-Saint Cloud, 1963-64; 1967-68; 1969-70.

Table A-3, which describes the female arrest rates for all crimes combined and for specific offense categories shows that in most of the countries female arrests have not increased between 1963 and 1970. Of the twenty-four countries listed, in less than seven is there a trend toward higher arrest rates among women.

When we compared female arrest rates for specific offense categories, we again failed to discern any trend toward higher rates from 1963 to 1970 in any of the categories for most of the countries. And those countries in which there was a trend could not be characterized as homogeneous by their predominant economic or social characteristics.

Table A-4 lists the female arrest rates for the three time periods for all crimes combined. The countries that have the highest female arrest rates for all crimes are a mixed lot of modern and traditional, Western and Eastern, with their economies and technologies more and less developed. They include Thailand, the West Indies, and Tunisia, together with West Germany, England, and France. Among those countries, there is considerable variation in women's roles and statuses.

The highest female arrest rates for financial and white-collar type offenses occur primarily among the most economically developed and technologically advanced countries. They are, of course, the countries in which women are likely to be represented in the commercial labor force in the highest proportions and are, therefore, likely to have the greatest opportunities for committing fraud and minor larceny. We also found that when we correlated female arrest rates for specific offense categories, the strongest relationship was between minor larceny and fraud, $r = .81$. The other correlations ranged from .58 for murder and major larceny to .24 for major and minor larceny. (Remember that as defined in this context, major larceny includes armed robbery, an offense that in the United States is usually included among the violent offenses.)

To conclude, we found that while high crime rates and high arrest rates are associated with more economically developed and technologically advanced societies, there was little relationship between the amount of *female* crime (as measured by female arrest rates for all crimes combined or for specific offense categories) and the level of economic development. We also found no significant relationship between *female* arrests and over-all volume of crime or volume of arrests among the different countries. Neither did we find that

Table A-4
Percentage of Women among All Arrests for All Crimes in Selected Countries, 1963, 1968 and 1970

Country	1963	1968	1970	Mean
West Indies	36.3	8.3	16.6	28.9
New Zealand	8.2	11.9	41.0	25.3
Thailand	12.3	16.4	23.4	17.3
Portugal	16.9	17.6	16.9	17.2
Burma	12.0	5.8	15.7	16.7
Germany	15.6	16.1	17.2	16.4
Luxembourg	23.6	12.3	14.4	16.2
France	11.6	13.3	15.9	13.8
Austria	14.3	13.6	13.6	13.8
England and Wales	14.0	13.4	13.2	13.5
Tunisia	13.1	12.2	13.2	12.8
Israel	11.4	13.6	11.1	12.1
Korea	9.2	12.6	10.9	11.5
Scotland	12.2	9.9	10.9	10.9
Netherlands	10.9	10.4	10.1	10.4
Ireland	12.1	9.6	9.0	10.1
Denmark	9.0	7.5	7.8	8.0
Monaco	5.9	5.7	10.5	7.5
Tanzania	6.0	7.4	7.2	6.9
Cyprus	6.9	8.3	5.1	6.7
Finland	7.0	6.6	6.3	6.6
Japan	2.8	8.5	2.5	4.6
Malawi	4.8	3.5	4.5	4.2
Hong Kong	3.4	2.6	2.7	3.0
Fiji	3.2	3.0	2.2	1.9
Bruni	2.5	1.3	2.2	1.9

Source: Adapted from *International Crime Statistics*, International Criminal Police Organization (Interpol) 92-Saint Cloud, 1963-64; 1967-68; 1969-70.

female arrest rates had increased between 1963 and 1970. Countries that had high female arrest rates for any type of financial crime had high rates for other types of white-collar crimes. The countries that had the highest female arrest rates for fraud and minor larceny were primarily countries in which a large proportion of the women were employed outside the homes in commercial occupations.

There was no relationship between countries that had high female arrest rates for violent offenses and those that had high female arrest rates for property or financial offenses.

The data in this appendix and the comments about them should have raised more questions about the extent and type of female involvement in crime in different societies than they answered. But having reached the era in which women are expected to be "into crime'' as they are expected to be ''into'' many activities that were previously closed or deemed inappropriate or of no interest to them, the topic of female participation in crime is one that should, and probably will, be explored in more depth in the next decade than it has been in the previous half century. Comparative studies of the type only suggested by the comments in this appendix should provide interesting and useful insights into women's propensities, capabilities, and behavior in criminal activities.

References

Arditi, R. R., F. Goldberg, Jr., M. M. Hartle, J. H. Peters, and W. R. Phelps. "The Sexual Segregation of American Prisons: Notes." 82 Yale Law Journal, 1229-73.

Blake, J. "Can We Believe Recent Data on Birth Expectations in the United States?" *Demography* 11, no. 1 (February 1974): 25-44.

Burkhart, K. *Women in Prison.* New York: Doubleday, 1973.

Chafe, W. H. *The American Woman.* New York: Oxford University Press, 1972.

Characteristics of New Commitments. State of New York, Department of Corrections, 1967, 1971.

Cowie, J., V. Cowie, and E. Slater. *Delinquency in Girls.* London: William Heinemann, Ltd., 1968.

Crime and Delinquency in California. Bureau of Criminal Statistics. Sacramento: Department of Justice, State of California, 1962.

Crime in California, 1952-1962. State of California, Department of Justice.

Crime in the United States, 1972. *Uniform Crime Reports.* U. S. Department of Justice.

Criminal Statistics, England and Wales. Presented to Parliament by the Secretary of State for the Home Department by Command of Her Majesty, July 1969, 1970, 1971. London: Her Majesty's Stationery Office.

deRham, E. *How Could She Do That?* New York: Clarkson N. Potter, 1969.

Epstein, C. and W. Goode (eds.). *The Other Half.* Englewood Cliffs, N.J.: Prentice Hall, Inc., 1971.

Erikson, E. *Identity, Youth and Crisis.* New York: W. W. Norton & Co., Inc., 1968.

Federal Offenders in the United States District Courts, 1963-1971. Washington, D.C.: Administrative Office of the U. S. Courts.

Ferriss, A. L. *Indicators of Trends in the Status of American Women.* New York: Russell Sage Foundation, 1971.

Freeman, J. "The Origins of the Women's Liberation Movement." *American Journal of Sociology* 78, no. 4 (January 1973): 798-812.

Giallombardo, R. *Society of Women: A Study of a Women's Prison*. New York: John Wiley and Sons, Inc., 1966.

Glueck, S., and E. Glueck. *Five Hundred Delinquent Women*. New York: Alfred A. Knopf, 1934.

Gornick, V. and B. Moran (eds.). *Women in Sexist Society*. New York: Basic Books, 1971.

International Crime Statistics. International Criminal Police Organization (Interpol), 92-St. Cloud, 1963-64; 1967-68; 1969-70.

Jenkins, E. *Six Criminal Women*. Freeport, N.Y.: Books for Libraries Press, 1949.

Klein, D. "The Etiology of Female Crime: A Review of the Literature." *Issues in Criminology* 8, no. 2 (Fall 1973): 3-29.

Konopka, G. *Adolescent Girls in Conflict*. Englewood Cliffs, N.J.: Prentice Hall, 1966.

Koontz, B. "Public Hearings on Women and Girl Offenders." *D.C. Commission on the Status of Women*, November 4, 1971.

Millett, K. *Prostitution Papers*. New York: Avon, 1973.

Millett, K. *Sexual Politics*. Garden City, N.Y.: W. W. Norton & Co., 1968.

Nagel, S. S. and L. J. Weitzman. "Women as Litigants." *The Hastings Law Journal* 23, no. 1 (November 1971): 171-98.

National Prisoners Statistics. Federal Bureau of Prisons, United States Department of Justice, 1972.

Ohio Judicial Criminal Statistics. Bureau of Statistics. Department of Mental Health and Mental Retardation, 1969, 1970, 1971.

Parker, T. *Women in Crime*. New York: Delacorte Press, 1965.

People in Prison, England and Wales. Presented to Parliament by the Secretary of State for the Home Department by Command of Her Majesty, November 1969. London: Her Majesty's Stationery Office.

Pollak, O. *The Criminality of Women*. Philadelphia: University of Pennsylvania Press, 1950.

Prisons and Borstals 1963, England and Wales. Presented to Parliament by the Secretary of State for the Home Department by Command of Her Majesty, June 1964. London: Her Majesty's Stationery Office.

Reckless, W. C. and B. A. Kay. *The Female Offenders*. Presidents

Commission on Law Enforcement and Administration of Justice, 1967.

Silverstein, L. *Defense of the Poor in Criminal Cases*. American Bar Foundation, 1965.

Singer, L. "Women and the Correctional Process." *American Criminal Law Review* 11:295, Winter 1973.

Sparrow, G. *Women Who Murder*. New York: Abelard-Schuman, 1970.

Statistical Abstracts of the United States, 1971. U. S. Department of Commerce, Bureau of Census.

Stimpson, C. "Is Women's Liberation a Lesbian Plot?" In Vivian Gornick and Barbara K. Moran (eds.). *Women in Sexist Society*. New York: Basic Books, 1971.

_____."'Thy Neighbor's Wife, Thy Neighbor's Servants': Women's Liberation and Black Civil Rights." In Vivian Gornick and Barbara K. Moran (eds.). *Woman in Sexist Society*. New York: Basic Books, 1971. pp. 622-657.

Temen, L. "Discriminatory Sentencing of Women Offenders" 11 *Criminal Law Review*, 1973.

Uniform Crime Reports, 1953-1972. Washington, D.C.: U.S. Federal Bureau of Investigation, United States Department of Justice.

Uniform Parole Reports. Davis, Calif.: National Council on Crime and Delinquency Research Center.

U.S. Census of Population, 1970. Subject Reports. Washington, D.C.: U. S. Dept. of Commerce, 1973.

Vedder, C. and D. Somerville. *The Delinquent Girl*. Springfield, Ill.: Charles C. Thomas, 1970.

Ward, D., M. Jackson, and E. Ward. "Crime and Violence by Women." *Crimes of Violence* 13, appendix 17. Presidents Commission on Law Enforcement and Administration of Justice, 1968.

Ward, D. and G. Kassebaum. *Women's Prisons*. Chicago: Aldine Publishing Co., 1965.

Watson, P. "Crime and Femininity." *The London Times*, July 22, 1973.

Index

About the Author

Rita James Simon is Professor of Law, Sociology, and Communications Research at the University of Illinois, on leave as Visiting Professor, Law School, Hebrew University, Jerusalem. After studies at the University of Wisconsin and Cornell University, Professor Simon received the Ph.D. from the University of Chicago. The author or editor of several books, the most recent being *The Jury System* (Sage Publications, 1975), Professor Simon has also written numerous articles, and is a member of several professional associations. She is the recipient of a Guggenheim Fellowship and a Ford Foundation Fellowship.